VISIBLE HERE and NOW

VISIBLE HERE
and NOW

The Buddha's Teachings on the
Rewards of Spiritual Practice

AYYA KHEMA

Translated by PETER HEINEGG
Edited by LEIGH BRASINGTON

With a translation of the
Sāmaññaphala Sutta by
BHIKKHU BODHI

SHAMBHALA
Boston & London
2001

Sʜᴀᴍʙʜᴀʟᴀ Pᴜʙʟɪᴄᴀᴛɪᴏɴs, Iɴᴄ.
Horticultural Hall
300 Massachusetts Avenue
Boston, Massachusetts 02115
www.shambhala.com

Fɪʀsᴛ Eᴅɪᴛɪᴏɴ
Printed in the United States of America

⊗ This edition is printed on acid-free paper that meets the
American National Standards Institute z39.48 Standard.
Distributed in the United States by Random House, Inc.,
and in Canada by Random House of Canada Ltd

Library of Congress Cataloging-in-Publication Data
Khema, Ayya.
[Früchte des spirituellen Lebens. English]
Visible here and now: the Buddha's teachings on the rewards of spiritual
practice / Ayya Khema; translated by Peter Heinegg; edited by Leigh Brasington;
with a translation of the Sâmaññaphala Sutta by Bhikkhu Bodhi.
p. cm.
ɪsʙɴ 1-57062-492-5
1. Spiritual life—Buddhism. 2. Meditation—Buddhism. 3. Reward
(Buddhism) I. Heinegg, Peter. II. Brasington, Leigh. III. Bodhi, Bhikkhu.
IV. Tipitaka. Suttapitaka. Dighanikaya. Samaññaphalasutta. English. V. Title.
BQ5612.K44413 2001
294.3'444—dc21
00-058328

CONTENTS

# Preface

When my teacher, the Reverend Ñānarāma Mahāthera, was asked once which of the many discourses of the Buddha he thought particularly important, he answered: the *Sāmaññaphala Sutta,* the discourse on the fruits of spiritual life. If you could get to know only one discourse, he explained, that should be the one. It contains the whole path of purification, meditation, and understanding that the Buddha taught and that leads to complete enlightenment.

So when we use this discourse (the second one in the long collection of the Buddha's discourses) as a guide for our spiritual development, it can shed a meaningful light on many questions that often seem difficult to us.

All those who have collaborated with me on this book and to whom I owe a debt of thanks will be happy if these explanations light up the way for a few men and women.

Ayya Khema
Buddha House
July 1997

Visible Here *and* Now

THE FRUITS of SPIRITUAL LIFE
Sāmaññaphala Sutta

Translated by BHIKKHU BODHI

THE STATEMENTS OF THE MINISTERS

1. Thus have I heard. On one occasion the Exalted One was dwelling at Rājagaha, in Jīvaka Komārabhacca's Mango Grove, together with a large company of twelve hundred and fifty bhikkhus. At the time, on the fifteenth-day Uposatha, the full-moon night of Komudi in the fourth month,* King Ajātasattu of Magadha, the son of Queen Videha, was sitting on the upper terrace of his palace surrounded by his ministers. There the king uttered the following joyful exclamation:

"How delightful, friends, is this moonlit night! How beautiful is this moonlit night! How lovely is this moonlit night! How tranquil is this moonlit night! How auspicious is this moonlit night! Is there any recluse or brahmin that we could visit tonight who might be able to bring peace to my mind?"

2. Thereupon one of his ministers said: "Your majesty, there is Pūraṇa Kassapa, the leader of an order, the leader of a group, the teacher of a group, well-known and famous, a spiritual leader whom many people esteem as holy. He is aged, long gone forth, advanced in years, in the last phase of life. Your majesty should visit him. Perhaps he might bring peace to your mind." But when this was said, King Ajātasattu remained silent.

*This would be the month of Kattika (October-November). The full-moon night of this month is called Komudī because it is said to be the time when the white water lily (kumuda) blooms.

3–7. Other ministers said: "Your majesty, there is Makkhali Go-sāla . . . Ajita Kesakambala . . . Pakudha Kaccāyana . . . Sañjaya Belaṭṭhaputta . . . Nigaṇṭha Nāṭaputta, the leader of an order, the leader of a group, well-known and famous, a spiritual leader whom many people esteem as holy. He is aged, long gone forth, advanced in years, in the last phase of life. Your majesty should visit him. Perhaps he might bring peace to your mind." But when this was said, King Ajātasattu remained silent.

THE STATEMENT OF JĪVAKA KOMĀRABHACCA

8. All this time Jīvaka Komārabhacca sat silently not far from King Ajātasattu. The king then said to him: "Friend Jīvaka, why do you keep silent?"

Jīvaka said: "Your majesty, the Exalted One, the Worthy One, the perfectly enlightened Buddha, together with a large company of twelve hundred and fifty bhikkhus, is now dwelling in our Mango Grove. A favorable report concerning him is circulating thus: 'This Exalted One is a worthy one, perfectly enlightened, endowed with clear knowledge and conduct, accomplished, a knower of the world, unsurpassed trainer of men to be tamed, teacher of gods and men, enlightened and exalted.' Your majesty should visit the Exalted One. Perhaps if you visit him he might bring peace to your mind."

9. "Then get the elephant vehicles prepared, friend Jīvaka." "Yes, your majesty!" Jīvaka replied. He then had five hundred female elephants prepared, as well as the king's personal bull-elephant, and announced to the king: "Your majesty, your elephant vehicles are ready. Do as you think fit."

10. King Ajātasattu then had five hundred of his women mounted on the female elephants, one on each, while he himself mounted his personal bull-elephant. With his attendants carrying torches, he went forth from Rājagaha in full royal splendor, setting out in the direction of Jīvaka's Mango Grove.

When King Ajātasattu was not far from the Mango Grove, he was suddenly gripped by fear, trepidation, and terror. Frightened, agitated, and terror-stricken, he said to Jīvaka: "You aren't deceiving me, are you friend Jīvaka? You aren't betraying me? You aren't about to turn me over to my enemies? How could there be such a large company of bhikkhus, twelve hundred and fifty bhikkhus, without any sound of sneezing or coughing, or any noise at all?"

"Do not be afraid, great king. Do not be afraid. I am not deceiving you, your majesty, or betraying you, or turning you over to your enemies. Go forward, great king! Go straight forward! Those are lamps burning in the pavilion hall."

THE QUESTION ON THE FRUITS OF RECLUSESHIP

11. Then King Ajātasattu, having gone by elephant as far as he could, dismounted and approached the door of the pavilion hall on foot. Having approached, he asked Jīvaka: "But where, Jīvaka, is the Exalted One?"

"That is the Exalted One, great king. He is the one sitting against the middle pillar, facing east, in front of the company of bhikkhus."

12. King Ajātasattu then approached the Exalted One and stood to one side. As he stood there surveying the company of bhikkhus, which sat in complete silence as serene as a calm lake, he uttered the following joyful exclamation: "May my son, the Prince Udāyibhadda, enjoy such peace as the company of bhikkhus now enjoys!"

[The Exalted One said:] "Do your thoughts, great king, follow the call of your affection?"

"Venerable sir, I love my son, the Prince Udāyibhadda. May he enjoy such peace as the company of bhikkhus now enjoys."

13. King Ajātasattu then paid homage to the Exalted One, reverently saluted the company of bhikkhus, sat down to one side, and said to the Exalted One: "Venerable sir, I would like to ask the Exalted One about a certain point, if he would take the time to answer my question."

"Ask whatever you wish to, great king."

14. "There are, venerable sir, various crafts, such as elephant trainers, horse trainers, charioteers, archers, standard bearers, camp marshals, commandos, high royal officers, front-line soldiers, bull-warriors, military heroes, mail-clad warriors, domestic slaves, confectioners, barbers, bath attendants, cooks, garland-makers, laundrymen, weavers, basket-makers, potters, statisticians, accountants, and various other crafts of a similar nature. All those [who practice these crafts] enjoy here and now the visible fruits of their craft. They obtain happiness and joy themselves, and they give happiness and joy to their parents, wives and children, and their friends and colleagues. They establish an excellent presentation of gifts to recluses and brahmins—leading to heaven, ripening in happiness, conducing to a heavenly rebirth. Is it possible, venerable sir, to point out any fruit of recluseship that is similarly visible here and now?"

15. "Do you remember, great king, ever asking other recluses and brahmins this question?"

"I do remember asking them, venerable sir."

"If it isn't troublesome for you, please tell us how they answered."

"It is not troublesome for me, venerable sir, when the Exalted One or anyone like him is present."

"Then speak, great king."

THE DOCTRINE OF PŪRAṆA KASSAPA

16. "One time, I approached Pūraṇa Kassapa, exchanged greetings and courtesies with him, and sat down to one side. I then asked him [in the same words as paragraph 14] if he could point out any fruit of recluseship visible here and now.

17. "When I had finished speaking, Pūraṇa Kassapa said to me: 'Great king, if one acts or induces others to act, mutilates or induces others to mutilate, tortures or induces others to torture, inflicts sorrow or induces others to inflict sorrow, oppresses or induces others to oppress, intimidates or induces others to intimidate; if he destroys life, takes what is not given, breaks into

houses, plunders wealth, commits burglary, ambushes highways, commits adultery, speaks falsehood—one does no evil. If with a razor-edged disk one were to reduce all the living beings on this earth to a single heap and pile of flesh, by doing so there would be no evil or outcome of evil. If one were to go along the south bank of the Ganges killing and inducing others to kill, mutilating and inducing others to mutilate, torturing and inducing others to torture, by doing so there would be no evil or outcome of evil. If one were to go along the north bank of the Ganges giving gifts and inducing others to give gifts, making offerings and inducing others to make offerings, by doing so there would be no merit or outcome of merit. By giving, self-control, restraint, and truthful speech there is no merit or outcome of merit.'

"Thus venerable sir, when I asked Pūraṇa Kassapa about a visible fruit of recluseship, he explained to me [his doctrine of] the inefficacy of action. Venerable sir, just as if one asked about a mango would speak about a breadfruit, or as if one asked about a breadfruit would speak about a mango, in the same way when I asked Pūraṇa Kassapa about a visible fruit of recluseship he explained to me [his doctrine of] the inefficacy of action. Then, venerable sir, I thought to myself: 'One like myself should not think of troubling a recluse or brahmin living in his realm.' So I neither rejoiced in the statement of Pūraṇa Kassapa, nor did I reject it. But though I neither rejoiced in it nor rejected it, I still felt dissatisfied, yet did not utter a word of dissatisfaction. Without accepting his doctrine, without embracing it, I got up from my seat and left.

THE DOCTRINE OF MAKKHALI GOSĀLA

18. "Another time, venerable sir, I approached Makkhali Gosāla, exchanged greetings and courtesies with him, and sat down to one side. I then asked him [as in paragraph 14] if he could point out a fruit of recluseship visible here and now.

19. "When I had finished speaking, Makkhali Gosāla said to me: 'Great king, there is no cause or condition for the defilement of

beings; beings are defiled without any cause or condition. There is no cause or condition for the purification of beings; beings are purified without cause or condition. There is no self-determination, no determination by others, no personal determination. There is no power, no energy, no personal strength, no personal fortitude. All sentient beings, all living beings, all creatures, all souls, are helpless, powerless, devoid of energy. Undergoing transformation by destiny, circumstance, and nature, they experience pleasure and pain in the six classes of men.

'There are fourteen hundred thousand principal modes of origin [for living beings] and six thousand [others] and six hundred [others]. There are five hundred kinds of kamma and five kinds of kamma and three kinds of kamma and full kamma and half-kamma. There are sixty-two pathways, sixty-two sub-aeons, six classes of men, eight stages in the life of man, forty-nine hundred modes of livelihood, forty-nine hundred kinds of wanderers, forty-nine hundred abodes of nāgas,* two thousand faculties, three thousand hells, thirty-six realms of dust, seven spheres of percipient beings, seven spheres of non-percipient beings, seven kinds of jointed plants, seven kinds of gods, seven kinds of human beings, seven kinds of demons, seven great lakes, seven major kinds of knots, seven hundred minor kinds of knots, seven major precipices, seven hundred minor precipices, seven major kinds of dreams, seven hundred minor kinds of dreams, eighty-four hundred thousand great aeons. The foolish and the wise, having roamed and wandered through these, will alike make an end to suffering.

'Though one might think: "By this moral discipline or observance or austerity or holy life I will ripen unripened kamma and eliminate ripened kamma whenever it comes up"—that cannot be. For pleasure and pain are measured out. Samsara's limits are fixed, and they can neither be shortened nor extended. There is no advancing forward and no falling back. Just as, when a ball of string is thrown, it rolls along unwinding until it comes to its

---

*Nāga: a dragon-like being in Indian mythology, supposed to dwell in the sea or beneath the earth.

end, in the same way, the foolish and the wise roam and wander [for the fixed length of time], after which they make an end to suffering.'

20. "Thus venerable sir, when I asked Makkhali Gosāla about a visible fruit of recluseship, he explained to me [his doctrine of] purification through wandering in samsara. Venerable sir, just as if one asked about a mango would speak about a breadfruit, or as if one asked about a breadfruit would speak about a mango, in the same way, when I asked Makkhali Gosāla about a visible fruit of recluseship, he explained to me [his doctrine of] purification through wandering in saṁsāra. Then, venerable sir, I thought to myself: 'One like myself should not think of troubling a recluse or brahmin living in his realm.' So I neither rejoiced in the statement of Makkhala Gosāla nor did I reject it. But though I neither rejoiced in it nor rejected it, I still felt dissatisfied, yet did not utter a word of dissatisfaction. Without accepting his doctrine, without embracing it, I got up from my seat and left.

THE DOCTRINE OF AJITA KESAKAMBALA

21. "Another time, venerable sir, I approached Ajita Kesakambala, exchanged greetings and courtesies with him, and sat down to one side. I then asked him [as in paragraph 14] if he could point out a fruit of recluseship visible here and now.

22. "When I had finished speaking, Ajita Kesakambala said to me: 'Great king, there is no giving, no offering, no liberality. There is no fruit or result of good and bad actions. There is no present world, no world beyond, no mother, no father, no beings who have taken rebirth. In the world there are no recluses and brahmins of right attainment who explain this world and the world beyond on the basis of their own direct knowledge and realization. A person is composed of the four primary elements. When he dies, the earth [in his body] returns to and merges with the [external] body of earth; the water [in his body] returns to and merges with the [external] body of water; the fire [in his body] returns to and merges with the [external] body of fire; the

air [in his body] returns to and merges with the [external] body of air. His sense faculties pass over into space. Four men carry the corpse along on a bier. His eulogies are sounded until they reach the charnel ground. His bones turn pigeon-colored. His meritorious offerings end in ashes. The practice of giving is a doctrine of fools. Those who declare that there is [an afterlife] speak only false, empty prattle. With the breaking up of the body, the foolish and the wise alike are annihilated and utterly perish. They do not exist after death.'

23. "Thus, venerable sir, when I asked Ajita Kesakambala about a visible fruit of recluseship, he explained to me [his doctrine of] annihilation. Venerable sir, just as if one asked about a mango would speak about a breadfruit, or as if one asked a breadfruit would speak about a mango, in the same way, when I asked Ajita Kesakambala about a visible fruit of recluseship, he explained to me [his doctrine of] annihilation. Then, venerable sir, I though to myself: 'One like myself should not think of troubling a recluse or brahmin living in his realm.' So I neither rejoiced in the statement of Ajita Kesakambala nor did I reject it. But though I neither rejoiced in it nor rejected it, I still felt dissatisfied; yet did not utter a word of dissatisfaction. Without accepting his doctrine, without embracing it, I got up from my seat and left.

THE DOCTRINE OF PAKUDHA KACCĀYANA

24. "Another time, venerable sir, I approached Pakudha Kaccāyana, exchanged greetings and courtesies with him, and sat down to one side. I then asked him [as in Paragraph 14] if he could point out a fruit of recluseship visible here and now.

25. "When I had finished speaking, Pakudha Kaccāyana said to me: 'Great king, there are seven bodies that are unmade, unfashioned, uncreated, without a creator, barren, stable as a mountain peak, standing firm like a pillar. They do not alter, do not change, do not obstruct one another; they are incapable of causing one another either pleasure or pain, or both pleasure and pain. What are the seven? The body of earth, the body of water,

the body of fire, the body of air, pleasure, pain, and the soul as the seventh. Among these there is no killer nor one who causes killing; no hearer nor one who causes hearing; no cognizer nor one who causes cognition. If someone were to cut off [another person's] head with a sharp sword, he would not be taking [the other's] life. The sword merely passes through the space between the seven bodies.'

26. "Thus, venerable sir, when I asked Pakudha Kaccāyana about a visible fruit of recluseship, he answered me in a completely irrelevant way. Venerable sir, just as if one asked about a mango would speak about a breadfruit, or as if one asked about a breadfruit would speak about a mango, in the same way, when I asked Pakudha Kaccāyana about a visible fruit of recluseship, he answered me in a completely irrelevant way. Then, venerable sir, I thought to myself: 'One like myself should not think of troubling a recluse or brahmin living in his realm.' So I neither rejoiced in the statement of Pakudha Kaccāyana nor did I reject it. But though I neither rejoiced in it nor rejected it, I still felt dissatisfied, yet did not utter a word of dissatisfaction. Without accepting his doctrine, without embracing it, I got up from my seat and left.

THE DOCTRINE OF NIGAṆṬHA NĀṬAPUTTA

27. "Another time, venerable sir, I approached Nigaṇṭha Nāṭaputta, exchanged greetings and courtesies with him, and sat down to one side. I then asked him [as in paragraph 14] if he could point out a fruit of recluseship visible here and now.

28. "When I had finished speaking, Nigaṇṭha Nāṭaputta said to me: "Great king, a Nigaṇṭha, a knotless one, is restrained with a fourfold restraint. How so? Herein, great king, a Nigaṇṭha is restrained with regard to all water; he is endowed with the avoidance of all evil; he is cleansed by the avoidance of all evil; he is suffused with the avoidance of all evil. Great king, when a Nigaṇṭha is restrained with this fourfold restraint, he is called a

knotless one who is self-perfected, self-controlled, and self-established.'

29. "Thus, venerable sir, when I asked Nigaṇṭha Nāṭaputta about a visible fruit of recluseship, he explained to me the fourfold restraint. Venerable sir, just as if one asked about a mango would speak about a breadfruit, or as if one asked about a breadfruit would speak about a mango, in the same way, when I asked Nigaṇṭha Nāṭaputta about a visible fruit of recluseship, he explained to me the fourfold restraint. Then, venerable sir, I thought to myself: 'One like myself should not think of troubling a recluse or brahmin living in his realm.' So I neither rejoiced in the statement of Nigaṇṭha Nāṭaputta nor did I reject it. But though I neither rejoiced in it nor rejected it, I still felt dissatisfied, yet did not utter a word of dissatisfaction. Without accepting his doctrine, without embracing it, I got up from my seat and left."

THE DOCTRINE OF SAÑJAYA BELAṬṬHAPUTTA

30. "Another time, venerable sir, I approached Sañjaya Belaṭṭhaputta, exchanged greetings and courtesies with him, and sat down to one side. I then asked him [as in paragraph 14] if he could point out any fruit of recluseship visible here and now.

31. "When I had finished speaking, Sañjaya Belaṭṭhaputta said to me: 'If you ask me:
A. 1. "Is there a world beyond?" if I thought that there is a world beyond I would declare to you, "There is a world beyond." But I do not say "It is this way," nor "It is that way," nor "It is otherwise." I do not say "It is not so," nor do I say "It is not not so."
'Similarly, you might ask me the following questions:
   2. "Is there no world beyond?"
   3. "Is it that there both is and is not a world beyond?"
   4. "Is it that there neither is nor is not a world beyond?"
B. 1. "Are there beings who have taken rebirth?"
   2. "Are there no beings who have taken rebirth?"

3. "Is it that there both are and are not beings who have taken rebirth?"

4. "Is it that there neither are nor are not beings who have taken rebirth?"

C. 1. "Is there fruit and result of good and bad actions?"

2. "Is there no fruit and result of good and bad actions?"

3. "Is it that there both are and are not fruit and result of good and bad actions?"

4. "Is it that there neither are nor are not fruit and result of good and bad actions?"

D. 1. "Does the Tathāgata exist after death?"

2. "Does the Tathāgata not exist after death?"

3. "Does the Tathāgata both exist and not exist after death?"

4. "Does the Tathāgata neither exist nor not exist after death?"

If I thought that it was so, I would declare to you "It is so." But I do not say "It is this way," nor "It is that way," nor "It is otherwise." I do not say "It is not so," nor do I say "It is not not so.'"

32. "Thus, venerable sir, when I asked Sañjaya Belaṭṭhaputta about a visible fruit of recluseship, he answer me evasively. Venerable sir, just as if one asked about a mango would speak about a breadfruit, or as if one asked about a breadfruit would speak about a mango, in the same way, when I asked Sañjaya Belaṭṭhaputta about a visible fruit of recluseship, he answered me evasively. Then, venerable sir, I though to myself: 'One like myself should not think of troubling a recluse or brahmin living in his realm.' So I neither rejoiced in the statement of Sañjaya Belaṭṭhaputta nor did I reject it. But though I neither rejoiced in it nor rejected it, I still felt dissatisfied, yet did not utter a word of dissatisfaction. Without accepting his doctrine, without embracing it, I got up from my seat and left.

THE FIRST VISIBLE FRUIT OF RECLUSESHIP

33. "So, venerable sir, I ask the Exalted One: There are, venerable sir, various crafts, such as elephant trainers, horse trainers,

charioteers, archers, standard bearers, camp marshals, commandos, high royal officers, front-line soldiers, bull-warriors, military
heroes, mail-clad warriors, domestic slaves, confectioners, barbers, bath attendants, cooks, garland-makers, laundrymen, weavers, basket-makers, potters, statisticians, accountants, and various
other crafts of a similar nature. All those [who practice these
crafts] enjoy here and now the visible fruit of their craft. They
obtain happiness and joy themselves, and they give happiness and
joy to their parents, wives and children, and their friends and
colleagues. They establish an excellent presentation of gifts to
recluses and brahmins—leading to heaven, ripening in happiness, conducing to a heavenly rebirth. Is it possible, venerable sir,
to point out any fruit of recluseship that is similarly visible here
and now?"

34. "It is, great king. But let me question you about this matter.
Answer as you think fit. What do you think, great king? Suppose
you have a slave, a workman who rises up before you, retires
after you, does whatever you want, acts always for your pleasure,
speaks politely to you, and is ever on the lookout to see that you
are satisfied. The thought might occur to him: 'It is wonderful
and marvelous, the destiny and result of meritorious deeds. For
this King Ajātasattu is a human being, and I too am a human
being, yet King Ajātasattu enjoys himself fully endowed and sup-
plied with the five strands of sense pleasure as if he were a god,
while I am his slave, his workman—rising before him, retiring
after him, doing whatever he wants, acting always for his pleasure, speaking politely to him, ever on the lookout to see that he
is satisfied. I could be like him if I were to do meritorious deeds.
Let me then shave off my hair and beard, put on saffron robes,
and go forth from the household life into homelessness. "After
some time he shaves off his hair and beard, puts on saffron robes,
and goes forth from the household life into homelessness. Having
gone forth, he dwells restrained in body, speech, and mind, content with the simplest food and shelter, delighting in solitude.
Suppose your men were to report all this to you. Would you say:
'Bring that man back to me, men. Let him again become my

slave, my workman, rising before me, retiring after me, doing whatever I want, acting always for my pleasure, speaking politely to me, ever on the lookout to see that I am satisfied'?"

35. "Certainly not, venerable sir. Rather, we would pay homage to him, rise up out of respect for him, invite him to a seat, and invite him to accept from us robes, almsfood, dwelling and medicinal requirements. And we would provide him righteous protection, defense, and security."

36. "What do you think, great king? If such is the case, is there or is there not a visible fruit of recluseship?"

"There certainly is, venerable sir."

"This, great king, is the first fruit of recluseship, visible here and now, that I point out to you."

THE SECOND VISIBLE FRUIT OF RECLUSESHIP

37. "Is it possible, venerable sir, to point out some other fruit of recluseship visible here and now?"

"It is, great king. But let me question you about this matter. Answer as you think fit."

"What do you think, great king? Suppose there is a farmer, a householder, who pays taxes to maintain the royal revenue. The thought might occur to him: 'It is wonderful and marvelous, the destiny and result of meritorious deeds. For this King Ajātasattu is a human being, and I too am a human being. Yet King Ajātasattu enjoys himself fully endowed with the five strands of sense pleasures as if he were a god, while I am a farmer, a householder, who pays taxes to maintain the royal revenue. I could be like him if I were to do meritorious deeds. Let me then shave off my hair and beard, put on saffron robes, and go forth from the household life into homelessness.'

"After some time, he abandons his accumulation of wealth, be it large or small, abandons his circle of relatives, be it large or small; he shaves off his hair and beard, puts on saffron robes, and goes forth from the household life into homelessness. Having gone forth, he dwells restrained in body, speech, and mind, content with the simplest food and shelter, delighting in solitude. Suppose your men were to report all this to you. Would you say: 'Bring that man back to me, men. Let him again become my slave, my workman, rising before me, retiring after me, doing whatever I want, acting always for my pleasure, speaking politely to me, ever on the lookout to see that I am satisfied'?"

38. "Certainly not, venerable sir. Rather, we would pay homage to him, rise up out of respect for him, invite him to a seat, and invite him to accept from us robes, almsfood, dwelling and medicinal requirements. And we would provide him righteous protection, defense, and security."

39. "What do you think, great king? If such is the case, is there or is there not a visible fruit of recluseship?"

"There certainly is, venerable sir."

"This, great king, is the second fruit of recluseship, visible here and now, that I point out to you."

THE MORE EXCELLENT FRUITS OF RECLUSESHIP

40. "Is it possible venerable sir, to point out any other fruit of recluseship visible here and now, more excellent and sublime than these two fruits?"

"It is possible. Listen, great king, and attend carefully. I will speak."

"Yes, venerable sir," King Ajātasattu replied to the Exalted One.

41. The Exalted One spoke: "Herein, great king, a Tathāgata arises in the world, a worthy one, perfectly enlightened, endowed with clear knowledge and conduct, accomplished, a knower of the world, unsurpassed trainer of men to be tamed, teacher of gods and men, enlightened and exalted. Having realized by his own direct knowledge this world with its gods, its Māras, and its Brahmās, this generation with its recluses and brahmins, its rulers and people, he makes it known to others. He teaches the

Dhamma that is good in the beginning, good in the middle, and good in the end, possessing meaning and phrasing; he reveals the holy life that is fully complete and purified.*

42. "A householder, or a householder's son, or one born into some other family, hears the Dhamma. Having heard the Dhamma, he gains faith in the Tathāgata. Endowed with such faith, he reflects: 'The household life is crowded, a path of dust. Going forth is like the open air. It is not easy for one dwelling at home to lead the perfectly complete, perfectly purified holy life, bright as a polished conch. Let me then shave off my hair and beard, put on saffron robes, and go forth from the household life into homelessness.'

43. "After some time he abandons his accumulation of wealth, be it large or small; he abandons his circle of relatives, be it large or small; he shaves off his hair and beard, puts on saffron robes, and goes forth from the household life into homelessness.

44. "When he has thus gone forth, he lives restrained by the restraint of the Pātimokkha,† possessed of proper behavior and resort. Having taken up the rules of training, he trains himself in them, seeing danger in the slightest faults. He comes to be endowed with wholesome bodily and verbal action, his livelihood is purified, and he is possessed of moral discipline. He guards the doors of his sense faculties, is endowed with mindfulness and clear comprehension, and is content.

THE SMALL SECTION ON MORAL DISCIPLINE

45. "And how, great king, is the bhikkhu possessed of moral discipline? Herein, great king, having abandoned the destruction

*In this translation the phrase "fully complete and purified" is construed as standing in apposition to "holy life," whereas the commentary (see below) takes it to stand in apposition to "Dhamma." The former interpretation seems to be borne out by section 42.
†The code of fundamental monastic rules, 227 in its Pali version.

of life, the bhikkhu abstains from the destruction of life. He has laid down the rod and weapon and dwells conscientious, full of kindness, sympathetic for the welfare of all living beings. This pertains to his moral discipline.

"Having abandoned taking what is not given, he abstains from taking what is not given. Accepting and expecting only what is given, he lives in honesty with a pure mind. This too pertains to his moral discipline.

"Having abandoned incelibacy, he leads the holy life of celibacy. He dwells aloof and abstains from the vulgar practice of sexual intercourse. This too pertains to his moral discipline.

"Having abandoned false speech, he abstains from falsehood. He speaks only the truth, he lives devoted to truth; trustworthy and reliable, he does not deceive anyone in the world. This too pertains to his moral discipline.

"Having abandoned slander, he abstains from slander. He does not repeat elsewhere what he has heard here in order to divide others from the people here, nor does he repeat here what he has heard elsewhere in order to divide these from the people there. Thus he is a reconciler of those who are divided and a promoter of friendships. Rejoicing, delighting, and exulting in concord, he speaks only words that are conducive to concord. This too pertains to his moral discipline.

"Having abandoned harsh speech, he abstains from harsh speech. He speaks only such words as are gentle, pleasing to the ear, endearing, going to the heart, polite, amiable and agreeable to the manyfolk. This too pertains to his moral discipline.

"Having abandoned idle chatter, he abstains from idle chatter. He speaks at the right time, speaks what is factual and beneficial, speaks on the Dhamma and the Discipline. His words are worth treasuring; they are timely, backed by reasons, measured, and connected with the good. This too pertains to his moral discipline.

"He abstains from damaging seed and plant life.

He eats only in one part of the day, refraining from food at night and from eating at improper times.

He abstains from dancing, singing, instrumental music, and from witnessing unsuitable shows.

He abstains from wearing garlands, embellishing himself with scents, and beautifying himself with unguents.

He abstains from high and luxurious beds and seats.

He abstains from accepting gold and silver.

He abstains from accepting uncooked grain, raw meat, women and girls, male and female slaves, goats and sheep, fowl and swine, elephants, cattle, horses and mares.

He abstains from accepting fields and lands.

He abstains from running messages and errands.

He abstains from buying and selling.

He abstains from dealing with false weights, false metals, and false measures.

He abstains from the crooked ways of bribery, deception, and fraud.

He abstains from mutilating, executing, imprisoning, robbery, plunder, and violence.

This too pertains to his moral discipline.

THE INTERMEDIATE SECTION ON MORAL DISCIPLINE

46. "Whereas some recluses and brahmins, while living on food offered by the faithful, continually cause damage to seed and plant life—to plants propagated from roots, stems, joints, buddings, and seeds—he abstains from damaging seed and plant life. This too pertains to his moral discipline.

47. "Whereas some recluses and brahmins, while living on food offered by the faithful, enjoy the use of stored-up goods, such as stored-up food, drinks, garments, vehicles, bedding, scents, and comestibles—he abstains from the use of stored-up goods. This too pertains to his moral discipline.

48. "Whereas some recluses and brahmins, while living on food offered by the faithful, attend unsuitable shows, such as:

shows featuring dancing, singing, or instrumental music;

theatrical performances;

ballad recitations;

music played by hand-clapping, cymbals, and drums;

art exhibitions;

acrobatic performances;

combats of elephants, horses, buffaloes, bulls, goats, rams, cocks, and quails;

staff-fights, boxing, and wrestling;

sham-fights, roll-calls, battle-arrays, and regimental reviews—he abstains from attending such unsuitable shows. This too pertains to his moral discipline.

49. "Whereas some recluses and brahmins, while living on food offered by the faithful, indulge in the following games and recreations,*

eight-row board games;

ten-row board games;

hopscotch;

spillikins;

dice;

stick games;

finger-painting;

ball games;

blowing through pipes;

playing with toy ploughs;

turning somersaults;

playing with toy windmills;

playing with toy measures;

playing with toy chariots;

playing with toy bows;

guessing letters;

guessing thoughts;

mimicking deformities—he abstains from such games and recreations. This too pertains to his moral discipline.

*The explanations of these games are drawn from the commentary.

50. "Whereas some recluses and brahmins, while living on food offered by the faithful, enjoy the use of high and luxurious beds and seats, such as:

spacious couches;

thrones with animal figures carved on the supports;

long-haired coverlets;

multicolored patchwork coverlets;

white woolen coverlets;

woolen coverlets embroidered with animal figures;

woolen coverlets with hair on both sides or on one side;

bedspreads embroidered with gems;

silk coverlets;

dance-hall carpets;

elephant, horse, or chariot rugs;

rugs of antelope-skins;

choice spreads made of kadali-deer hides;

spreads with red awnings overhead;

couches with red cushions for the head and feet—he abstains from the use of such high and luxurious beds and seats. This too pertains to his moral discipline.

51. "Whereas some recluses and brahmins, while living on the food offered by the faithful, enjoy the use of such devices for embellishing and beautifying themselves as the following: rubbing scented powders into the body, massaging with oils, bathing in perfumed water, kneading the limbs, mirrors, ointments, garlands, scents, unguents, face powders, make-up, bracelets, headbands, decorated walking sticks, ornamented medicine-tubes, rapiers, sunshades, embroidered sandals, turbans, diadems, yak-tail whisks, and long-fringed white robes—he abstains from the use of such devices for embellishment and beautification. This too pertains to his moral discipline.

52. "Whereas some recluses and brahmins, while living on the food offered by the faithful, engage in frivolous chatter, such as: talk about kings, thieves, and ministers of state; talk about armies, dangers, and wars; talk about food, drink, garments, and

lodgings; talk about garlands and scents; talk about relations, vehicles, villages, towns, cities, and countries; talk about women
and talk about heroes; street talk and talk by the well; talk about
those departed in days gone by; rambling chit-chat; speculations
about the world and about the sea; talk about gain and loss—he
abstains from such frivolous chatter. This too pertains to his
moral discipline.

53. "Whereas some recluses and brahmins, while living on the
food offered by the faithful, engage in wrangling argumentation,
[saying to one another]:
   'You don't understand this doctrine and discipline. It is I who
understand this doctrine and discipline.'
   'How can you understand this doctrine and discipline?'
   'You're practicing the wrong way. I'm practicing the right
way,'
   'I'm being consistent. You're inconsistent.'
   'What should have been said first you said last, what should
have been said last you said first.'
   'What you took so long to think out has been confuted.'
   'Your doctrine has been refuted. You're defeated. Go, try to
save your doctrine, or disentangle yourself now if you can'—
he abstains from such wrangling argumentation. This too pertains to his moral discipline.

54. "Whereas some recluses and brahmins, while living on the
food offered by the faithful, engage in running messages and errands, for kings, ministers of state, khattiyas, brahmins, house-
holders, or youths, [who command them]: 'Go here, go there,
take this, bring that from there'—he abstains from running such
messages and errands. This too pertains to his moral discipline.

55. "Whereas some recluses and brahmins, while living on the
food offered by the faithful, engage in scheming, talking, hinting,
belittling others, and pursuing gain with gain, he abstains from
such kinds of scheming and talking.* This too pertains to his
moral discipline.

*Improper ways of gaining material support from donors, discussed in detail in
Vism., 1.61–82, pp. 24–30.

56. "Whereas some recluses and brahmins, while living on the food offered by the faithful, earn their living by a wrong means of livelihood, by such debased arts as:*

prophesying long life, prosperity, etc., or the reverse, from the marks on a

person's limbs, hands, feet, etc.;

divining by means of omens and signs;

making auguries on the basis of thunderbolts and celestial portents;

interpreting ominous dreams;

telling fortunes from marks on the body;

making auguries from the marks on cloth gnawed by mice;

offering fire oblations;

offering oblations from a ladle;

offering oblations of husks, rice powder, rice grains, ghee and oil to the gods;

offering oblations from the mouth;

offering blood-sacrifices to the gods;

making predictions based on the fingertips;

determining whether the site for a proposed house or garden is propitious or not;

making predictions for officers of state;

laying demons in a cemetery;

laying ghosts;

knowledge of charms to be pronounced by one living in an earthen house;

snake charming;

the poison craft, scorpion craft, rat craft, bird craft, crow craft;

foretelling the number of years that a man has to live;

reciting charms to give protection from arrows;

reciting charms to understand the language of animals—

he abstains from such wrong means of livelihood, from such debased arts. This too pertains to his moral discipline.

*The explanation of these arts, usually indicated by a single obscure word in the text, is drawn from the commentary.

57. "Whereas some recluses and brahmins, while living on the food offered by the faithful, earn their living by a wrong means of livelihood, by such debased arts as interpreting the significance of the color, shape, and other features of the following items to determine whether they portend fortune or misfortune for their owners: gems, garments, staffs, swords, spears, arrows, bows, other weapons, women, men, boys, girls, slaves, slave-women, elephants, horses, buffaloes, bulls, cows, goats, rams, fowl, quails, iguanas, earrings [or house-gables], tortoises, and other animals—he abstains from such wrong means of livelihood, from such debased arts. This too pertains to his moral discipline.

58. "Whereas some recluses and brahmins, while living on the food offered by the faithful, earn their living by a wrong means of livelihood, by such debased arts as making predictions to the effect that:

the king will march forth;
the king will return;
our king will attack and the enemy king will retreat;
the enemy king will attack and our king will retreat;
our king will triumph and the enemy king will be defeated;
the enemy king will triumph and our king will be defeated;
thus there will be victory for one and defeat for the other—
he abstains from such wrong means of livelihood, from such debased arts. This too pertains to his moral discipline.

59. "Whereas some recluses and brahmins, while living on the food offered by the faithful, earn their living by a wrong means of livelihood, by such debased arts as predicting: there will be an eclipse of the moon, an eclipse of the sun, an eclipse of a constellation; the sun and the moon will go on their proper courses; there will be an aberration of the sun and moon; the constellations will go on their proper courses; there will be an aberration of a constellation; there will be a fall of meteors; there will be a sky-blaze; there will be an earthquake; there will be an earth-roar; there will be a rising and setting, a darkening and brightening, of the moon, sun, and constellations; such will be the result of the moon's eclipse, such the result of the sun's eclipse, [and so

on down to] such will be the result of the rising and setting, darkening and brightening, of the moon, sun, and constellations—he abstains from such wrong means of livelihood, from such debased arts. This too pertains to his moral discipline.

60. "Whereas some recluses and brahmins, while living on the food offered by the faithful, earn their living by a wrong means of livelihood, by such debased arts as predicting: there will be abundant rain; there will be a drought; there will be a good harvest; there will be a famine; there will be security; there will be danger; there will be sickness; there will be health; or they earn their living by accounting, computation, calculation, the composing of poetry, and speculations about the world—he abstains from such wrong means of livelihood, from such debased arts. This too pertains to his moral discipline.

61. "Whereas some recluses and brahmins, while living on the food offered by the faithful, earn their living by a wrong means of livelihood, by such debased arts as: arranging auspicious dates for marriages, both those in which the bride is brought home and those in which she is sent out; arranging auspicious dates for betrothals and divorces; arranging auspicious dates for the accumulation or expenditure of money; reciting charms to make people lucky or unlucky; rejuvenating the fetuses of abortive women; reciting spells to bind a man's tongue, to paralyze his jaws, to make him lose control over his hands, or to bring on deafness; obtaining oracular answers to questions by means of a mirror, a girl, or a god; worshiping the sun; worshiping Mahābrahmā; bringing forth flames from the mouth; invoking the goddess of luck—he abstains from such wrong means of livelihood, from such debased arts. This too pertains to his moral discipline.

62. "Whereas some recluses and brahmins, while living on the food offered by the faithful, earn their living by a wrong means of livelihood, by such debased arts as: promising gifts to deities in return for favors; fulfilling such promises; demonology; reciting spells after entering an earthen house; inducing virility and

impotence; preparing and consecrating sites for a house; giving ceremonial mouthwashes and ceremonial bathing; offering sacrificial fires; administering emetics, purgatives, expectorants, and phlegmagogues; administering ear-medicine, eye-medicine, nose-medicine, collyrium, and counter-ointments; curing cataracts, practicing surgery, practicing as a children's doctor; administering medicines to cure bodily diseases and balms to counter their after-effects—he abstains from such wrong means of livelihood, from such debased arts. This too pertains to his moral discipline.

63. "Great king, the bhikkhu who is thus possessed of moral discipline sees no danger anywhere in regard to his restraint by moral discipline. Just as a head-anointed noble warrior who has defeated his enemies sees no danger anywhere from his enemies, so the bhikkhu who is thus possessed of moral discipline sees no danger anywhere in regard to his restraint by moral discipline. Endowed with this noble aggregate of moral discipline, he experiences within himself a blameless happiness. In this way, great king, the bhikkhu is possessed of moral discipline.

RESTRAINT OF THE SENSE FACULTIES

64. "And how, great king, does the bhikkhu guard the doors of his sense faculties? Herein, great king, having seen a form with the eye, the bhikkhu does not grasp at the sign or the details. Since, if he were to dwell without restraint over the faculty of the eye, evil unwholesome states such as covetousness and grief might assail him, he practices restraint, guards the faculty of the eye, and achieves restraint over the faculty of the eye. Having heard a sound with the ear . . . having smelled an odor with the nose . . . having tasted a flavor with the tongue . . . having touched a tangible object with the body . . . having cognized a mind-object with the mind, the bhikkhu does not grasp at the sign or the details. Since, if he were to dwell without restraint over the faculty of the mind, evil unwholesome states of covetousness and grief might assail him, he practices restraint, guards the faculty of the mind. Endowed with this noble restraint of

the sense faculties, he experiences within himself an unblemished happiness. In this way, great king, the bhikkhu guards the doors of the sense faculties.

MINDFULNESS AND CLEAR COMPREHENSION

65. "And how, great king, is the bhikkhu endowed with mindfulness and clear comprehension? Herein, great king, in going forward and returning, the bhikkhu acts with clear comprehension. In looking ahead and looking aside, he acts with clear comprehension. In bending and stretching his limbs, he acts with clear comprehension. In wearing his robes and cloak and using his almsbowl, he acts with clear comprehension. In eating, drinking, chewing, and tasting, he acts with clear comprehension. In defecating and urinating, he acts with clear comprehension. In going, standing, sitting, lying down, waking up, speaking, and remaining silent, he acts with clear comprehension. In this way, great king, the bhikkhu is endowed with mindfulness and clear comprehension.

CONTENTMENT

66. "And how, great king, is the bhikkhu content? Herein, great king, a bhikkhu is content with robes to protect his body and almsfood to sustain his belly; wherever he goes he sets out taking only [his requisites] along with him. Just as a bird, wherever it goes, flies with its wings as its only burden, in the same way a bhikkhu is content with robes to protect his body and almsfood to sustain his belly; wherever he goes he sets out taking only [his requisites] along with him. In this way, great king, the bhikkhu is content.

THE ABANDONING OF THE HINDRANCES

67. "Endowed with this noble aggregate of moral discipline, this noble restraint over the sense faculties, this noble mindfulness and clear comprehension, and this noble contentment, he resorts

to a secluded dwelling—a forest, the foot of a tree, a mountain, a glen, a hillside cave, a cremation ground, a jungle grove, the open air, a heap of straw. After returning from his alms-round, following his meal, he sits down, crosses his legs, holds his body erect, and sets up mindfulness before him.

68. "Having abandoned covetousness for the world, he dwells with a mind free from covetousness; he purifies his mind from covetousness. Having abandoned ill will and hatred, he dwells with a benevolent mind, sympathetic for the welfare of all living beings; he purifies his mind from ill will and hatred. Having abandoned dullness and drowsiness, he dwells perceiving light, mindful and clearly comprehending; he purifies his mind from dullness and drowsiness. Having abandoned restlessness and worry, he dwells at ease within himself, with a peaceful mind; he purifies his mind from restlessness and worry. Having abandoned doubt, he dwells as one who has passed beyond doubt, unperplexed about wholesome states; he purifies his mind from doubt.

69. "Great king, suppose a man were to take a loan and apply it to his business, and his business were to succeed, so that he could pay back his old debts and would have enough money left over to maintain a wife. He would reflect on this, and as a result he would become glad and experience joy.

70. "Again, great king, suppose a man were to become sick, afflicted, gravely ill, so that he could not enjoy his food and his strength would decline. After some time he would recover from that illness and would enjoy his food and regain his bodily strength. He would reflect on this, and as a result he would become glad and experience joy.

71. "Again, great king, suppose a man were locked up in a prison. After some time he would be released from prison, safe and secure, with no loss of his possessions. He would reflect on this, and as a result he would become glad and experience joy.

72. "Again, great king, suppose a man were a slave, without independence, subservient to others, unable to go where he wants.

After some time he would be released from slavery and gain his independence; he would no longer be subservient to others but a free man able to go where he wants. He would reflect on this, and as a result he would become glad and experience joy.

73. "Again, great king, suppose a man with wealth and happiness and possessions were traveling along a desert road where food was scarce and dangers were many. After some time he would cross over the desert and arrive safely in a village that is safe and free from danger. He would reflect on this, and as a result he would become glad and experience joy.

74. "In the same way, great king, when a bhikkhu sees that these five hindrances are unabandoned within himself, he regards that as a debt, as a sickness, as confinement in prison, as slavery, as a desert road.

75. "But when he sees that these five hindrances have been abandoned within himself, he regards that as freedom from debt, as good health, as release from prison, as freedom from slavery, as a place of safety.

76. "When he sees that these five hindrances have been abandoned within himself, gladness arises. When he is gladdened, rapture arises. When his mind is filled with rapture, his body becomes tranquil; tranquil in body, he experiences happiness; being happy, his mind becomes concentrated.

The First Jhāna

77. "Quite secluded from sense pleasures, secluded from unwholesome states, he enters and dwells in the first jhāna, which is accompanied by applied and sustained thought and filled with the rapture and happiness born of seclusion. He drenches, steeps, saturates, and suffuses his body with this rapture and happiness born of seclusion, so that there is no part of his entire body that is not suffused by this rapture and happiness.

78. "Great king, suppose a skilled bath attendant or his apprentice were to pour soap-powder into a metal basin, sprinkle it with

water, and knead it into a ball, so that the ball of soap powder would be pervaded by moisture, encompassed by moisture, suffused with moisture inside and out, yet would not trickle. In the same way, great king, the bhikkhu drenches, steeps, saturates, and suffuses his body with the rapture and happiness born of seclusion so that there is no part of his entire body which is not suffused by this rapture and happiness. This, great king, is a visible fruit of recluseship more excellent and sublime than the previous ones.

The Second Jhāna

79. "Further, great king, with the subsiding of applied and sustained thought, the bhikkhu enters and dwells in the second jhāna, which is accompanied by internal confidence and unification of mind, is without applied and sustained thought, and is filled with the rapture and happiness born of concentration. He drenches, steeps, saturates, and suffuses his body with this rapture and happiness born of concentration, so that there is no part of his entire body which is not suffused by this rapture and happiness.

80. "Great king, suppose there were a deep lake whose waters welled up from below. It would have no inlet for water from the east, west, north, or south, nor would it be refilled from time to time with showers of rain; yet a current of cool water, welling up from within the lake, would drench, steep, saturate, and suffuse the whole lake, so that there would be no part of that entire lake which is not suffused with the cool water. In the same way, great king, the bhikkhu drenches, steeps, saturates, and suffuses his body with the rapture and happiness born of concentration, so that there is no part of his entire body which is not suffused by this rapture and happiness. This too, great king, is a visible fruit of recluseship more excellent and sublime than the previous ones.

THE THIRD JHĀNA

81. "Further, great king, with the fading away of rapture, the bhikkhu dwells in equanimity, mindful and clearly comprehending, and experiences happiness with the body. Thus he enters and dwells in the third jhāna, of which the noble ones declare: 'He dwells happily with equanimity and mindfulness.' He drenches, steeps, saturates, and suffuses his body with this happiness free from rapture, so that there is no part of his entire body which is not suffused by this happiness.

82. "Great king, suppose in a lotus pond there were blue, white, or red lotuses that have been born in the water, grow in the water, and never rise up above the water, but flourish immersed in the water. From their tips to their roots they would be drenched, steeped, saturated, and suffused with cool water, so that there would be no part of those lotuses not suffused with cool water. In the same way, great king, the bhikkhu drenches, steeps, saturates, and suffuses his body with the happiness free from rapture, so that there is no part of his entire body which is not suffused by this happiness. This too, great king, is a visible fruit of recluseship more excellent and sublime than the previous ones.

THE FOURTH JHĀNA

83. "Further, great king, with the abandoning of pleasure and pain, and with the previous passing away of joy and grief, the bhikkhu enters and dwells in the fourth jhāna, which is neither pleasant nor painful and contains mindfulness fully purified by equanimity. He sits suffusing his body with a pure bright mind, so that there is no part of his entire body not suffused by a pure bright mind.

84. "Great king, suppose a man were to be sitting covered from the head down by a white cloth, so that there would be no part of his entire body not suffused by the white cloth. In the same

way, great king, the bhikkhu sits suffusing his body with a pure bright mind, so that there is no part of his entire body not suffused by a pure bright mind. This too, great king, is a visible fruit of recluseship more excellent and sublime than the previous ones.

Insight Knowledge

85. "When his mind is thus concentrated, pure and bright, unblemished, free from defects, malleable, wieldy, steady, and attained to imperturbability, he directs and inclines it to knowledge and vision. He understands thus: 'This is my body, having material form, composed of the four primary elements, originating from father and mother, built up out of rice and gruel, impermanent, subject to rubbing and pressing, to dissolution and dispersion. And this is my consciousness, supported by it and bound up with it.'

86. "Great king, suppose there were a beautiful beryl green gem of purest water, eight faceted, well cut, clear, limpid, flawless, endowed with all excellent qualities. And through it there would run a blue, yellow, red, white, or brown thread. A man with keen sight, taking it in his hand, would reflect upon it thus: 'This is a beautiful beryl gem of purest water, eight faceted, well cut, clear, limpid, flawless, endowed with all excellent qualities. And running through it there is this blue, yellow, red, white, or brown thread.' In the same way, great king, when his mind is thus concentrated, pure and bright . . . the bhikkhu directs and inclines it to knowledge and vision and understands thus: 'This is my body, having material form . . . and this is my consciousness, supported by it and bound up with it.' This too, great king, is a visible fruit of recluseship more excellent and sublime than the previous ones.

The Knowledge of the Mind-made Body

87. "When his mind is thus concentrated, pure and bright, unblemished, free from defects, malleable, wieldy, steady, and at-

tained to imperturbability, he directs and inclines it to creating a mind-made body. From this body, he creates another body having material form, mind-made, complete in all its parts, not lacking any faculties.

88. "Great king, suppose a man were to draw out a reed from its sheath. He would think: 'This is the reed; this is the sheath. The reed is one thing, the sheath another, but the reed has been drawn out from the sheath.' Or suppose a man were to draw a sword out from its scabbard. He would think: 'This is the sword; this is the scabbard. The sword is one thing, the scabbard another, but the sword has been drawn out from the scabbard.' Or suppose a man were to pull a snake out from its slough. He would think: 'This is the snake; this is the slough. This snake is one thing; the slough another, but the snake has been pulled out from the slough.' In the same way, great king, when his mind is thus concentrated, pure and bright . . . the bhikkhu directs and inclines it to creating a mind-made body. From this body he creates another body having material form, mind-made, complete in all its parts, not lacking any faculties. This too, great king, is a visible fruit of recluseship more excellent and sublime than the previous ones.

The Knowledge of the Modes of Supernatural Power

89. "When his mind is thus concentrated, pure and bright, unblemished, free from defects, malleable, wieldy, steady, and attained to imperturbability, he directs and inclines it to the modes of supernormal power. He exercises the various modes of supernormal power: having been one, he becomes many and having been many, he becomes one; he appears and vanishes; he goes unimpeded through walls, ramparts, and mountains as if through space; he dives in and out of the earth as if it were water; he walks on water without sinking as if it were earth; sitting cross-legged he travels through space like a winged bird; with his hand he touches and strokes the sun and the moon, so

mighty and powerful; he exercises mastery over the body as far as the Brahmā-world.

90. "Great king, suppose a skilled potter or his apprentice were to make and fashion out of well-prepared clay whatever kind of vessel he might desire. Or suppose a skilled ivory-worker or his apprentice were to make and fashion out of well-prepared ivory whatever kind of ivory work he might desire. Or suppose a skilled goldsmith or his apprentice were to make and fashion out of well-prepared gold, whatever kind of gold work he might desire. In the same way, great king, when his mind is thus concentrated, pure and bright . . . the bhikkhu directs and inclines it to the modes of supernormal power and exercises the various modes of supernormal power. This too, great king, is a visible fruit of recluseship more excellent and sublime than the previous ones.

The Knowledge of the Divine Ear

91. "When his mind is thus concentrated, pure and bright, unblemished, free from defects, malleable, wieldy, steady, and attained to imperturbability, he directs and inclines it to the divine ear-element. With the divine ear-element, which is purified and surpasses the human, he hears both kinds of sound, the divine and the human, those which are distant and those which are near.

92. "Great king, suppose a man traveling along a highway were to hear the sounds of kettledrums, tabors, horns, cymbals and tomtoms, and would think: 'This is the sound of kettledrums, this the sound of tabors, this the sound of horns, cymbals and tomtoms.' In the same way, great king, when his mind is thus concentrated, pure and bright . . . the bhikkhu directs and inclines it to the divine ear-element. With the divine ear-element, which is purified and surpasses the human, he hears both kinds of sound, the divine and the human, those which are distant and those which are near. This too, great king, is a visible fruit of recluseship more excellent and sublime than the previous ones.

The Knowledge of Encompassing the Minds of Others

93. "When his mind is thus concentrated, pure and bright, unblemished, free from defects, malleable, wieldy, steady, and attained to imperturbability, he directs and inclines it to the knowledge of encompassing the minds [of others]. He understands the minds of other beings and persons, having encompassed them with his own mind. He understands a mind with lust as a mind with lust and a mind without lust as a mind without lust; he understands a mind with hatred as a mind with hatred and a mind without hatred as a mind without hatred; he understands a mind with delusion as a mind with delusion and a mind without delusion as a mind without delusion; he understands a contracted mind as a contracted mind and a distracted mind as a distracted mind; he understands an exalted mind as an exalted mind and an unexalted mind as an unexalted mind; he understands a surpasssable mind as a surpassable mind and an unsurpassable mind as an unsurpassable mind; he understands a concentrated mind as a concentrated mind and an unconcentrated mind as an unconcentrated mind; he understands a liberated mind as a liberated mind and an unliberated mind as an unliberated mind.

94. "Great king, suppose a young man or woman, fond of ornaments, examining his or her own facial reflection in a pure bright mirror or in a bowl of clear water, would know, if there were a mole, 'It has a mole,' and if there were no mole, 'It has no mole.' In the same way, great king, when his mind is thus concentrated, pure and bright . . . the bhikkhu directs and inclines it to the knowledge of encompassing the minds [of others]. He understands the minds of other beings and persons, having encompassed them with his own mind. This too, great king, is a visible fruit of recluseship more excellent and sublime than the previous ones.

95. "When his mind is thus concentrated, pure and bright, un-blemished, free from defects, malleable, wieldy, steady, and at-tained to imperturbability, he directs and inclines it to the knowledge of recollecting past lives. He recollects his numerous past lives, that is, one birth, two births, three, four, or five births; ten, twenty, thirty, forty, or fifty births; a hundred births, a thou-sand births, a hundred thousand births; many aeons of world contraction, many aeons of world expansion, many aeons of world contraction and expansion, [recollecting]: 'There I had such a name, belonged to such a clan, had such an appearance; such was my food, such my experience of pleasure and pain, such my span of life. Passing away from that state, I re-arose there. There too I had such a name, belonged to such a clan, had such an appearance; such was my food, such my experience of pleasure and pain, such my span of life. Passing away from that state I re-arose here.' Thus he recollects his numerous past lives in their modes and their details.

96. "Great king, suppose a man were to go from his own village to another village, then from that village to still another village, and then from that village he would return to his own village. He would think to himself: 'I went from my own village to that village. There I stood in such a way, sat in such a way, spoke in such a way, and remained silent in such a way. From that village I went to still another village. There too I stood in such a way, sat in such a way, spoke in such a way, and remained silent in such a way. From the village I returned to my own village.' In the same way, great king, when his mind is thus concentrated, pure and bright . . . the bhikkhu directs and inclines it to the knowledge of recollecting past lives, and he recollects his numer-ous past lives in their modes and their details. This too, great king, is a visible fruit of recluseship, more excellent and sublime than the previous ones.

97. "When his mind is thus concentrated, pure and bright, unblemished, free from defects, malleable, wieldy, steady, and attained to imperturbability, he directs and inclines it to the knowledge of the passing away and re-appearance of beings. With the divine eye, which is purified and surpasses the human, he sees beings passing away and re-appearing—inferior and superior, beautiful and ugly, fortunate and unfortunate—and he understands how beings fare according to their kamma, thus: 'These beings—who were endowed with bad conduct of body, speech, and mind, who reviled the noble ones, held wrong views, and undertook actions governed by wrong views—with the breakup of the body, after death, have re-appeared in the plane of misery, the bad destinations, the lower realms, in hell. But these beings—who were endowed with good conduct of body, speech, and mind, who did not revile the noble ones, held right views, and undertook actions governed by right views—with the breakup of the body, after death, have reappeared in the good destinations, in the heavenly world.' Thus with the divine eye, which is purified and surpasses the human, he sees beings passing away and re-appearing—inferior and superior, beautiful and ugly, fortunate and unfortunate—and he understands how beings fare in accordance with their kamma.

98. "Great king, suppose in a central square there were a building with an upper terrace, and a man with keen sight standing there were to see people entering a house, leaving it, walking along the streets, and sitting in the central square. He would think to himself: 'Those people are entering the house, those are leaving it, those are walking along the streets, and those are sitting in the central square.' In the same way, great king, when his mind is thus concentrated, pure and bright . . . the bhikkhu directs and inclines it to the knowledge of the arising and passing away of beings. With the divine eye, which is purified and surpasses the human, he sees beings passing away and re-appearing,

and he understands how beings fare according to their kamma. This too, great king, is a visible fruit of recluseship more excellent and sublime than that previous ones.

THE KNOWLEDGE OF THE DESTRUCTION OF THE CANKERS

99. "When his mind is thus concentrated, pure and bright, unblemished, free from defects, malleable, wieldy, steady, and attained to imperturbability, he directs and inclines it to the knowledge of the destruction of the cankers. He understands as it really is: "This is suffering.' He understands as it really is: 'This is the origin of suffering.' He understands as it really is: 'This is the cessation of suffering.' He understands as it really is: 'This is the way leading to the cessation of suffering.' He understands as it really is: 'These are the cankers.' He understands as it really is: 'This is the origin of the cankers.' He understands as it really is: 'This is the cessation of the cankers.' He understands as it really is: 'This is the way leading to the cessation of the cankers.'

"Knowing and seeing thus, his mind is liberated from the canker of sensual desire, from the canker of existence, and from the canker of ignorance. When it is liberated, the knowledge arises: 'It is liberated.' He understands: 'Destroyed is birth, the holy life has been lived, what had to be done has been done, there is nothing further beyond this.'

100. "Great king, suppose in a mountain glen there were a lake with clear water, limpid and unsullied. A man with keen sight, standing on the bank, would see oyster-shells, sand and pebbles, and shoals of fish moving about and keeping still. He would think to himself: 'This is a lake with clear water limpid and unsullied, and there within it are oyster-shells, sand and pebbles, and shoals of fish moving about and keeping still.'

"In the same way, great king, when his mind is thus concentrated, pure and bright . . . the bhikkhu directs and inclines it to the knowledge of the destruction of the cankers. He understands as it really is: 'This is suffering.' . . . He understands: 'Destroyed is birth, the holy life has been lived, what had to be done has been done, there is nothing further beyond this.' This too, great king, is a visible fruit of recluseship more excellent and sublime than the previous ones. And, great king, there is no other fruit of recluseship higher or more sublime than this one."

KING AJĀTASATTU DECLARES HIMSELF A LAY FOLLOWER

101. When the Exalted One had finished speaking, King Ajāta-sattu said to him: "Excellent, venerable sir! Excellent, venerable sir! Just as if one were to turn upright what had been turned upside down, or to reveal what was hidden, or to point out the right path to one who was lost, or to bring a lamp into a dark place so that those with keen sight could see forms, in the same way, venerable sir, the Exalted One has revealed the Dhamma in numerous ways. I go for refuge to the Exalted One, to the Dhamma, and to the Bhikkhu Sangha. Let the Exalted One accept me as a lay follower gone for refuge from this day onward as long as I live.

"Venerable sir, a transgression overcame me. I was so foolish, so deluded, so unskillful that for the sake of rulership I took the life of my own father, a righteous man and a righteous king. Let the Exalted One acknowledge my transgression as a transgression for the sake of my restraint in the future."

102. "Indeed, great king, a transgression overcame you. You were so foolish, so deluded, so unskillful that for the sake of rulership you took the life of your father, a righteous man and a righteous king. But since you have seen your transgression as a transgression and make amends for it according to the Dhamma, we acknowledge it. For, great king, this is growth in the discipline of the Noble One: that a person sees his transgression as a transgression, makes amends for it according to the Dhamma, and achieves restraint in the future."

103. When this was said, King Ajātasattu said to the Exalted One: "Now, venerable sir, we must go. We have many tasks and duties."

"Do whatever seems fit, great king."

Then King Ajātasattu rejoiced in the word of the Exalted One and thanked him for it. Rising from his seat, he paid homage to the Exalted One, circumambulated him, and departed.

104. Soon after King Ajātasattu had left, the Exalted One addressed the bhikkhus: "This king, bhikkhus, has ruined himself; he has injured himself. Bhikkhus, if this king had not taken the life of his father, a righteous man and a righteous king, then in this very seat there would have arisen in him the dust-free, stainless eye of Dhamma."

Thus spoke the Exalted One. Elated in mind, the bhikkhus rejoiced in the Exalted One's word.

Here ends the *Sāmaññaphala Sutta*.

1. THE FIRST THREE FRUITS OF THE SPIRITUAL LIFE

THE DISCOURSE BEGINS on a night of a full moon, with King Ajātasattu sitting with his retinue and his ministers on the terrace of his palace. He asks those present whether anyone knows of a priest or monk who could help him find inner peace. Everyone praises and recommends one teacher or another, but the king already knows them all. The conversation is mostly about six spiritual teachers whom the king has already visited. None had been able to help him. Only one of the company sits and holds his tongue: the king's personal physician. The king turns to him, and Jīvaka reports to him about the Buddha, who just now happens to be in his mango grove.

At this the king immediately has the elephants saddled, for he wishes to ride to Jīvaka's mango grove. And so, according to tradition, five hundred elephants are saddled for the five hundred wives of the king. If he were to put men on the elephants, it would look as if he were setting off to war, and then he might be exposed to attacks along the way. Ajātasattu has the reputation of a great warrior. He supposedly conquered so much land around his state of Magadha that it served as the core of a great Indian empire.

And so with great pomp they ride to the mango grove; but in the end they have to proceed on foot, because the path becomes too narrow for so large a group. Jīvaka had reported that twelve hundred and fifty monks were staying with the Buddha. But when they come closer, they can't hear a sound. Perfect quiet prevails. This seems rather strange to the king, and in his concern he asks Jīvaka: "Are you sure you haven't lured me into a trap? How can so large a community, twelve hundred and fifty monks, be gathered without making a sound?" As a warrior, he had judged others by his own standards—as we all do—and considered how he himself would have staged such a situation. But Jīvaka calms him with the words: "Lamps are burning there at the pavilion."

Thus the king approaches the Buddha with his retinue and his personal physician; he sits down and asks if he may propose a question. The Buddha immediately agrees—most of his discourses were prompted by questions.

The question that the king asks the Buddha deals with what we are basically looking for when we sense that material life alone doesn't satisfy us. Ajātasattu wants to know where the "visible profit" lies for anyone who devotes himself to the spiritual life.

The Buddha asks whether he has already put this question to other teachers and what they have answered. The expositions by the six teachers may have been woven into the discourse at a later date, since they take up so much space. In any case they're interesting because they come from teachers who were famous at the time and had many followers.

One of them, the king reports to the Buddha, said that it made no difference at all what one did, because individual actions had no results. Everything that happens in life is simply fate. If this were true, there would be no spiritual growth. If everything is fate anyway, then meditation is superfluous, because we can't change anything that happens. If our actions, which can be good, bad, or neutral, lead to no results, we needn't strive for the good. In that case whatever we do would be inconsequential. But in principle we know this isn't true. We experience happiness and unhappiness, and often enough we recognize what led us to get the results that we got. Thus, without having asked anyone about it, we know this can't be right.

Nevertheless, two teachers argue for this doctrine. The third teacher claims that a person is just a body and that with the death of the body the person disappears. The fourth explains that a person has a body and a soul, and that the soul is immortal, remaining forever the way it is. That would mean that we are separate individuals for all eternity, stuck forever with the same difficulties.

The next teacher holds that the only important thing is moral behavior—which the Buddha too sees as the foundation of the spiritual life. But this teacher points out no further steps.

The last teacher is such a thorough skeptic that he can't fully profess anything. On every subject he says more or less: "If that's how it is, then that's how it is; and if it's otherwise, then it'll be otherwise." He delivers a long speech saying as much.

Meanwhile the king's pangs of conscience are causing him extraordinary difficulties. Regret and self-blame are nothing new to us either. We're familiar with both of them; and we've often experienced how they won't let us rest—even if it's not quite a matter of patricide, as it was with King Ajātasattu.

Thus, after the king has given a detailed answer to the Buddha's question about what he heard from the six teachers, the Buddha describes the various possibilities for profiting from a life of renunciation.

The two first "fruits" that the Buddha points out to the king have a wholly concrete and material connection to life in India at the time. The Buddha says that the king should imagine a palace slave who works for him all day long and is always at his beck and call. One day this man abandons his home, his work, all his material security. He embarks on the path of a spiritual seeker and lives on whatever people give him. How would the king feel about him? Would he try to get him back? The king replies: No, of course not. He would support the man.

Even today it's customary in India for those who are on a spiritual quest to be supported by others. The Buddha further asks whether this is a visible fruit of renunciation, and the king says it is.

Those who are searching for spiritual truth no longer need to be at others' beck and call or work for them. They will surely be supported by the people they meet.

Next, the Buddha says that the king should imagine a farmer who works hard and pays taxes. One day this farmer decides that he wants to find spiritual truth. He gives up his work and heads off into the unknown. He goes from house to house with his alms bowl, begging for food, and dedicates himself entirely to spiritual growth. Would the king fetch him back?

The king replies that of course he wouldn't; rather he would support him. The Buddha declares that this is a second fruit of renunciation, already visible in one's lifetime.

But the king still isn't satisfied, because the Buddha himself had never been a palace slave, nor did he ever have to work in the fields. He was a prince and had set off on the path of renunciation. Hence the king would like to know whether there isn't an even greater profit, a more visible gain. What he means is: you did things differently—there has to be something more impressive. The Buddha then explains that this is in fact true.

If one dedicates one's life to the spiritual path, the next thing one gains is an inner trust in the teaching that the Buddha called *dhamma* (Skt. *dharma*). The word *dhamma* has various meanings. First of all, it means the teaching of the Buddha. Then it refers to the law, the law of nature, the truth, what really is. The Buddha wanted to help human beings recognize how things really are. So he told the king: if one takes the path of renunciation—if one identifies totally with the spiritual life and devotes oneself to it, one will gain confidence in the highest ideal.

What humans experience every day, what they have to deal with, is material things. Like that farmer, they have to earn money. They have to take care of their body and their family. They have to keep their house and property in order and constantly repair things, which are constantly falling apart. So they don't have much time or energy to do anything else. We can see with our own eyes the profit made by following a profession or trade: the beautiful house, the healthy people—all material things. But this can't lead to trust, since we have to work for everything, and everything keeps passing away. In addition, we are afraid that everything we have created may be lost, or that we may get no recognition. And the knowledge that we can't rely one hundred percent on anyone except ourselves (and even that only in a limited way) engenders fear. There's a lack of trust, and the opposite of trust is fear and insecurity, which shape our life, because it's so transitory. We are all filled with uncertainty, although we try to whitewash all this with the things that preoccupy us.

The Buddha teaches the king as follows: we can leave all this behind us and devote ourselves to the spiritual life only when we have gained trust. Trust is the foundation of the heart. Thanks to it we feel safe and unassailable, because we know that there is something much loftier than material life.

The Buddha rejected blind faith and spoke of a trust that was meant to be paired with wisdom. He offered a simile: trust, he said, was like a blind giant, and wisdom like a sharp-eyed cripple. The blind giant asks the sharp-eyed cripple: "Come, ride on my shoulders. I'm strong, but I can't see well. You're weak, but you've got sharp eyes. Together we can go a long way."

This means that if we have trust in the teaching and in the teacher, it shouldn't rest on blind faith. Blind faith is, to be sure, very strong and can move mountains; but when it's conditioned by blindness, you don't know which mountain should be moved. We need wisdom here, so that thanks to our intelligence we can discern what the teaching is about. We cannot practice without trust, because only trust opens up the heart. By contrast, when we let it dominate us, the rational mind keeps finding more and more counterarguments, and it becomes impossible to transcend the world. There's always something to find fault with. Above all, with their critical intellect, Westerners keep discovering new points to criticize. On the material level there are defects and problems everywhere.

That's why trust is indispensable for the opening of the heart, which alone leads to devotion. We can compare this to learning how to swim. People who don't know how to swim are afraid; they lack trust that the water will bear them up. They also lack trust that the swimming teacher's advice is right. If we don't give ourselves completely to the teacher's directions and the water, we'll never learn how to swim.

When trust and devotion are lacking on the spiritual plane, every practice goes wrong. It's an absolute precondition that we dedicate ourselves wholeheartedly and follow the instructions.

The mind that understands what is at stake, why we practice, and what is important, must do its share. Thus we need heart and mind to practice effectively: a heart that is devoted and a mind that understands. If we don't practice seeing clearly, then we have what in India is called *bhakti*: total devotion to the human or divine guru. This awakens love and creates a feeling of protection, of untouchability, because one has given oneself to something higher, but it's not oriented to understanding.

The Buddha was a pioneer precisely on this level. As early as this period, *bhakti* was treasured and practiced in India. But the Buddha taught that we need both devotion and insight, which are equivalent to heart and understanding. Our first step is the opening of the heart, because without it the mind creates too many difficulties. We practiced the art of debate in school; we've been able to do it since we were children. It's a popular social game nowadays, and politicians play it masterfully. But if the heart opens to spiritual growth, to the knowledge that there is an absolute truth, then it will want to approach that truth and will be able to give itself so fully to the truth that it will also be ready to try the Path. That's what it's all about: trying things out for oneself.

This can be compared to the taste of a mango. Someone who has never eaten one might ask, "Why are you buying a mango? How does it taste?" To which the answer will be, "It tastes sweet; it's juicy and soft." If we have never tasted a mango, we might imagine the taste of a peach. But once we have tasted a mango, we don't have to ask about it. So we need enough trust to try the things out ourselves.

On the spiritual path we need time and patience with ourselves. Patience is also a part of love. A mother has patience with her children. We have to learn to be our own mother and our own child, so that we can develop patience with our difficulties. Everything changes anyway, uninterruptedly. If we are convinced that we wish to dedicate our life to spiritual growth, then it will change in that direction. Wherever we direct our mind, that's where it goes. The Buddha often recommended directing the mind to absolute truth and not waiting until the day when insight comes calling. If we turn our mind to spiritual under-standing, it has the possibility of adapting to that. If we direct it, for example, to detective stories or gangster movies, it will adapt to them. If we direct it to spiritual ideals, to trust, to experience of the self, it will dedicate itself to that. The more often we do it, the easier we'll find it. At first the mind is often stubborn, because it's used to always doing just what it likes; but gradually it becomes more and more capable of adapting.

Trust also helps us to develop self-confidence. We absolutely need this in the spiritual life; otherwise we can easily fall prey to obsessive doubt. Trust in oneself is not the same thing as arro-gance. People with no self-confidence often think that someone who has it is arrogant, because one recognizes only one's mirror image. The opposite of self-confidence is an inferiority complex. Self-confidence, by contrast, is a feeling of security, a rock-solid inner conviction that you will be up to whatever may come.

Self-confidence is strengthened by meditation. Yet we also need self-confidence to practice meditation in the first place. We can recognize ourselves as children of the universe with a right to be here, not overwhelmed with difficulties but a part of nature. This creates a sense of inner ease that simplifies meditation. Inner heaviness makes meditation difficult.

There is surely not a single person whose daily life always runs the way he or she would like. We always encounter other people who have ideas exactly contrary to ours. It's a constant interplay, and we feel burdened because we continually strive to put our environment in order, although there is nothing to be put in order. The other people are the way they are. The only thing that can be put in order is ourselves.

Once we have become familiar with inner ease, we also recog-nize its cause. We have let go of much of our own striving, and are just there. Then we can also trust the totality that surrounds us and doesn't threaten us. We feel threatened only when we isolate ourselves. Self-confidence, trust in ourselves, is a spiritual quality that we need for practice and that we can continue to deliberately strengthen until one day it will be anchored in us and stay put.

We have reason to be thankful, because more than twelve hundred years ago the Indian sage and scholar Padmasambhava, who brought Buddhism to Tibet, made the following prophecy: "When the iron eagle flies and horses run on wheels, the Tibetan people will be scattered over the world like ants and the dhamma will come to the land of the red man."

The "iron eagle," is, of course, the airplane; the "horses on wheels" jam our highways, and the "red man" refers to the pink skin of Western Caucasians. The jewel of the dhamma, whose value we may not be able to appreciate until we fasten it in our hearts, is offered to our Western culture. That's why trust is so crucial.

2. THE FOURTH FRUIT
Moral Behavior

EVEN AFTER THE BUDDHA TEACHES King Ajātasattu about trust, the king still isn't satisfied and asks for an even more visible gain. He sees trust as a good and helpful quality but fails to realize that it's comparable to the gain that accrues from material life, and hence he wishes to learn still more.

Thereupon the Buddha answers, Yes, there is an even more concrete kind of gain to be found as a fruit of renunciation: the virtuous behavior of a person who attributes great value to morality. Then the Buddha explains that it is profitable not to expose oneself to the dangers of creating bad *kamma* (Skt. *karma*), not to be burdened with regrets, not to blame oneself, not to feel pangs of guilt, and hence to be inwardly happy.

This applies exactly to the king, who feels massive remorse and who wishes to hear more on the subject. So the Buddha continues: above all, the five precepts must be followed; they form, so to speak, the foundation for a good human life. Although these precepts sound obvious and simple, they are hard to maintain. Hence the Buddha also explains that they are a form of training. He doesn't say that we'll be punished if we don't keep them, but says that we should put these precepts into practice.

The first precept is that one should never kill living creatures. This refers, of course, not just to human beings—even though the king, who has murdered his own father, must feel quite personally addressed by that. But there is more than not killing to this first of the five precepts that have to be kept by everyone who wishes to follow a spiritual path. One must also practice the opposite: loving-kindness, compassion, and harmlessness on all levels. Killing is cruel and hateful; it relates, in the first instance, to the body. There is also the emotional and mental level. Being harmless means not only not killing, but also being careful and considerate, and dealing with other living creatures as we wish to be treated.

When we think of love, we have ideas that are purely personal and, on the whole, quite fanciful. They are based in general on our desire to be loved, from which we expect fulfillment. In reality love fulfills only the one who loves. If we understand love as a quality of the heart, just as intelligence is a quality of the mind, then we won't deal with love as people customarily do. As a rule we discriminate, judge, and condemn and limit ourselves to giving our love where we see a chance of being loved in return, and when we consider someone lovable. But no one who is not fully enlightened—and that means all of us—is totally lovable. Looking for someone who is absolutely worthy of love is wasted effort. We divide our hearts into different compartments, for lovable, neutral, and unlovable people. With that sort of divided heart, there's no way we can feel good. We can be "whole" only with a heart united in love.

Being loved is in principle nothing more than a confirmation of ego, because it proves to us that despite everything we are worthy of love. However, if someone who loves us should happen at any time to change his or her mind—which is always possible and even permissible—then we suddenly cease to feel lovable. Meanwhile nothing at all has changed except someone else's opinion.

Often we find ourselves torn. The things that we do generate our own kamma; they make us happy or unhappy. What others do is their kamma, and if we make ourselves dependent on them, we are like slaves who have to take orders. But if we trust in our own capacity to love—and everyone has that—and try to cultivate it, we become free and independent. Then it's no longer important whether somebody loves us. It's very gratifying, should it happen, for the person whose heart is full of love. But the main thing is that we ourselves feel love.

When we have developed love, we are incapable of killing. It even becomes impossible to cause emotional pain. The discomfort that we experience when our relationships are not harmonious and peaceful becomes stronger than our fear of death. The love that the Buddha spoke of is called *mettā* in Pali. We translate this as "loving-kindness" because it includes both kindness and love. There is a considerable difference between what we call love and what the Buddha characterized as mettā. In general we speak about love in a personal relationship, which always presupposes a dependency. The other must be present, and love us, and always react the way we want him or her to. Since we know very well that anything like this is impossible, this kind of love is always matched with fear and hence is not pure. In this context one cannot speak of "true" love.

True love exists when the heart is so broadly trained that it can embrace all human beings and all living creatures. This requires a learning process that is sometimes hard, above all when someone turns out to be very unfriendly or unpleasant. But this condition can be reached by everyone, because we all have the capacity for love within us.

Every moment that we spend on the training of our hearts is valuable and brings us a step further along the path of purification. The more often we remember that all our heart has to do is love, the easier it will be to distance ourselves from judgments and condemnations. But that doesn't mean we can no longer distinguish between good and evil. If we couldn't do that, our moral concepts would get muddled and we wouldn't be able to keep the precepts. Naturally we know what is evil, but hatred of evil needn't forever be stirring in our heart. On the contrary, we have compassion for those who act in a way that does harm.

The spiritual path is a path of the purification of heart and mind. We can use every opportunity for it and need never interrupt this learning process. Every time we get a chance to practice what is beneficial, we'll feel a sense of relief. Hating, rejecting, getting irritated is burdensome and depressing. It's impossible to be happy when you're angry. Being happy when we love is quite simple. Unfortunately we have a false notion of loving. Deep down we believe that it means being loved. Dropping this idea is itself a process of purification and an exercise in letting go.

For spiritual growth "letting go" is the most important term to attend to. The further we take this path of purification, the simpler our life becomes. The more we cling, the harder it gets. Just imagine how people try to snatch up an endless variety of things, to grasp at them and hold them tight. Something is forever coming loose and escaping from their grip, so they have to bend to pick it up. Then the next thing escapes. With so many things to hold on to, this becomes hard and uncomfortable. One day a person says: "Enough!"—and drops everything. What happens next? Quite simply, one no longer needs to bend down and no longer feels burdened. Unfortunately we know that this isn't so easy. Everyone around us is clutching things, and so we think we have to do the same. But as soon as we have tried and found out how simple it is to let go, we'll see the blessing in it. There is none greater.

There was a meditation teacher from Thailand whose simple, practical method of explanation won him many disciples, even though he couldn't speak English. One peculiar feature of Westerners is that they never stop asking questions. And so Ajahn Chah was asked one day, "You keep saying that we shouldn't cling to anything, that we should let go of everything. But you have lots of things here in your own hut. Besides that, you have a monastery and many disciples. How can that be?" Ajahn Chah answered with a counterquestion: "Do you see this glass full of water on the table?" The questioner said yes. "Now," the master explained, "from this glass I can drink water when I'm thirsty. And it's a very beautiful glass, which I once got as a present. Nevertheless, for me the glass is already broken in pieces."

It's actually quite simple. As long as the glass hasn't been broken, it remains useful and one can enjoy it. Still, it's quite certain that at some point it will be broken, because everything is transitory. But Ajahn Chah wouldn't be sad about the glass, because for him it was already broken. We should always be aware of this fact. Then we won't find it hard to let go, so that the fear of inevitable loss disappears. If we have learned above all to let go of our opinion of ourselves, there won't be any more problems. If, whenever we look at anything, we think that nothing lasts, we'll be able to let go and thus be on the way of purification. Regret, hatred, and craving have no more targets when we know how exhausting it is to cling to them.

It's the same with love: as long as we have a claim on possession, there will be problems. But if we look at everything as if it were already broken in pieces, we'll realize that nothing else is important except purifying our emotions. Because one thing is indisputable: everything will break, everything will change, and every mind that is thinking about something definite will soon be thinking about something else.

Our emotions cloud our minds, and there can't be clarity until the emotions are purified. So long as we are overwhelmed by our emotions, we are busy only with them. We can compare this to the waves in the ocean: so long as we find ourselves in the middle of the waves, we see only the water that touches us. Not until the surface of the sea has been smoothed can we see into the depths and make out what's on the ocean floor. Our minds can't get any depth perspective until rest has come into our heart.

The second precept says that one shouldn't take what hasn't been given. It forbids stealing in a comprehensive sense; that is, we are not to take anything that isn't explicitly intended for us. The opposite of this is generosity and openhandedness based on love. If we don't love, then neither do we have the need to do good to others, and we can't give anything. Loving, consideration, and generosity shrink our ego. The goal of all practice is to recognize that the "I" is just an illusion. But the road to that realization is a long one, and we have to take many little steps to get there. What bars us from inner peace is this "I," the ego, which keeps on having wishes, which constantly wants to be confirmed and strengthened. It wants to assert itself at all times. When others are well disposed, it's glad; but if it picks up signals of rejection and criticism from outside, anger and displeasure arise within us. Loving for the sake of loving, giving for the sake of giving, to make others happy, helps to reduce our ego a little. It's only a matter of practice for us to keep directing our mind toward love and generosity; we can soon make a habit of it. The

Buddha said, "If it weren't possible to do only good, I wouldn't recommend it to you. It is possible."

Here we should consider that we don't do the work of purification for others, but first and foremost for ourselves. Of course, others will profit from it, but that's a secondary result.

Loving-kindness and generosity help us to recognize that in reality there are no boundary lines. Everything is connected to everything else. One cannot lead a satisfied life if one completely fences oneself off. If conflict and strife prevail, then we find ourselves in a state of war, and life becomes very hard and joyless. Therefore we have to learn to accept everyone, because he or she has the same cares and troubles as we do.

Once we've realized that we have to rely on one another, it's much simpler to be generous; and we can live together peacefully and harmoniously. The joy we bring another then becomes our own experience, something we have consciously striven for.

The third precept tells us not to act sexually in a way that brings harm to others. This precept doesn't refer exclusively to sexual relations, although these are often especially difficult, but to human relations in general. First a friend, then an enemy, calumnies and intrigues—that's the way it goes. We won't strive to fully develop fidelity, uprightness, and reliability until we've acknowledged that we ourselves are responsible for everything that happens. Thus we learn to trust ourselves, to be able to rely on ourselves; and this will also have a beneficial effect on our relations with one another.

The fourth precept is especially important. It insists on no falsity in speech. The Buddha often repeated the directive of right speech. It's one of the steps on the Eightfold Path, as well as one of the factors that bring happiness, as described in the discourse of the Great Blessing (*Maha-mangala Sutta,* SN II. 4 and Khp 5). Noble speech is so important because normally we speak all day long. Even if we don't talk out loud, our mind chatters away uninterruptedly and disturbs us. The right speech that the Buddha means doesn't depend upon our being elegant talkers. Once again this is a capacity that we can develop. The Buddha has given us a model of what right speech is and isn't.

If you know something that is not helpful and untrue, then do not say it.

If you know something that might be helpful but is untrue, do not say that either.

Even if you know something that is not helpful and true, do not speak about it.

But if you know something that is helpful and true, then find the right time to say it.

So we have to guard against blurting out anything impulsively and unreflectively. We have to wait for the right moment. But what is the right moment? That moment has come when we sense complete loving-kindness toward our interlocutor.

If we cherish anger, everything that we say is useless, because it simply won't get through to the other person. This means that the choice of words isn't so crucial. It all depends on the feeling that accompanies them. If it's one of sincere affection, then a successful conversation will take place. The choice of the right moment is closely linked to our emotions.

This is something we should and can learn. Obviously only true speech can also be right speech. The Buddha also called for avoiding arguments, manipulation, coarse language, and backbiting, while always striving for the truth that comes from the heart.

The spoken word itself plays a relatively small part in communication. Emotions, body language, facial expressions, and voice stamp our speech to a much greater extent than we commonly realize.

Right speech is a great blessing, because it avoids not just lying and slander, but also overstatement and understatement. It prevents gossip and useless chatter. Useless gossip is a very popular social game. Asking about how someone is doing is empty talk unless we're really interested in the answer. Talking about the weather, politics, or TV programs is for the most part idle chatter.

But then what do we have left that's worth discussing? A great, wide, vital territory—namely dhamma. In a society that knows nothing about the Buddha and dhamma, this certainly won't be easy. Nevertheless we can try to direct conversations along paths that are of general importance—for example, how to train the mind and open the heart. We mustn't forget that the conversations we habitually engage in are what feed our mind.

Surely we all take pains to give our body clean and healthy food. What's preventing us from doing the same with the mind? Nothing but a lack of mindfulness. Keeping the precepts is by no means as simple as it sounds. It's a spiritual undertaking. We sense a strong feeling of happiness when we know that we have tried our best.

The fifth and last precept says that we shouldn't consume any intoxicating beverages or drugs, because they make the mind more confused than it is already. Only mindfulness will help us to live in accordance with the precepts.

There's a story that fits in here, which tells of a monk who after twenty-four years concluded that over all that time he had made no spiritual progress worth mentioning. He was so depressed and desperate that he decided to end his life. He got a thick rope, climbed up a tree, tied the rope around a sturdy branch, and put the noose around his neck. Just as he was about to jump, it occurred to him that over all those twenty-four years he had never broken a single one of the many precepts to which he had bound himself. This knowledge filled him with such a powerful rush of happiness that he at once climbed down the tree and went on with his practice. The feeling of happiness made it possible for him to achieve such a concentrated meditation that after a few years he reached enlightenment.

This story shows that the feeling of happiness issuing from one's own discipline is the basis for the spiritual path. Those who always do their best to maintain discipline will ultimately get to know this feeling of happiness, of having conquered themselves. Self-discipline creates a certain control over mind and body, which also makes it possible to control the mind in meditation. Only a mind that does what we expect of it is under control, and can be led to where we want it to go, at the moment we choose, and for as long as we think right.

LOVING-KINDNESS CONTEMPLATION

This exercise differs from loving-kindness meditation (see page 98) because in it we actually consider and reflect, while in loving-kindness meditation the essential point is to experience the feeling. In contemplation the idea is to enter into ourselves, to get to know ourselves better. By contrast, meditation has the goal of sharpening our concentration. At first we direct our attention to the breath and speak the following words:

May I be free from enmity.

In order to contemplate that, we must look into our heart to see if there is any hostility in it. If there is, then we have to check whether this hostile attitude is of any use to us—whether it helps us to find happiness and peace. If not, we can try, on the strength of our understanding, to let go of and change these negative sensations. If something is of no use to us, we don't need to keep it.

May I not harm any living being.

Here, too, we have to check to see whether we have caused any bodily or emotional harm. The latter is by no means rare. This means that we have to make an effort not to do any harm, not to insist so much on our own point of view, and to avoid hurting others by arguments.

May I be free from mental and bodily difficulties.

Here we have to examine how we deal with our own difficulties, and whether we can't solve them. This isn't simple because we already have some deeply engrained behavior patterns. But we can change the mental difficulties and thereby create more free space and unencumbered spirit.

May I be capable of protecting my own happiness.

It's necessary to inspect carefully the actual contents of our own happiness, if we are to protect it at all.

May all living beings be free from hostility.

If at the beginning, when we contemplated our own hostility, we found a way to let it go, then it may be possible to communicate this solution to others and extend it to them. But first we have to find the success in ourselves.

May all beings not harm one another.

Again we wish for others what we have already discovered in ourselves, namely, that non-injury and readiness to help bring far more happiness than aggressive, self-righteous behavior does. Hence we wish that others too may acknowledge this.

May all beings be free from mental and bodily difficulties.

This too is something we've already examined for ourselves, and because it's important for us, we wish it for all others without distinction, even those who are indifferent to us or with whom we don't get along very well.

May all beings be capable of guarding their happiness.

Contemplation can show us that other people perceive happiness differently from ourselves. Even if we disagree, we can help them to guard their happiness.

3. THE FIFTH FRUIT
Limiting and Guarding Sense Contacts

THE FOUR GREAT EFFORTS

KING AJĀTASATTU HAS NOW HEARD from the Buddha what fruits the path of renunciation presents us with, namely the possibility of giving up domestic and professional life, of gaining trust, and of practicing moral behavior. But the king wants to know more, so the Buddha explains the next steps to him.

These steps gradually strengthen spirituality and support the process of purification. However, there has to be continuous practice, because living a life that does as little harm as possible demands real determination and constant recollection of moral behavior. As a help on this path Buddha mentions the limiting of sensory contacts. This is a very interesting step, and it too presupposes a firm decision.

In Buddhism thinking is considered one of the senses. Thus we have at our disposal six senses: hearing, seeing, smelling, tasting, touching, and thinking. We are continuously occupied with these six senses. Sensory contacts are our world. We have no others, until through meditation we become capable of reaching new levels of consciousness. The Buddha was once asked: "What is the universe?" His answer: "Seeing, hearing, smelling, tasting, touching, and thinking—that is the universe."

All sensory contacts are immediately followed by a feeling; it couldn't be otherwise. If we see something, a feeling arises at once. If what we have seen is pleasant, the subsequent feeling will be pleasant. And conversely, if we see something unpleasant, the feeling will be followed by a hostile reaction, for example: "That's horrible. I don't want it. Get it out of here!" But should the feeling be "wonderful," it will immediately prompt a desire to have something. Every reaction, therefore, will bring in its wake rejection or a wish for possession. Both fall under the rubric of desire, which is why at each moment we bind ourselves anew to the wheel of birth and death.

To understand this fatal process, we first have to grasp it intellectually and then live it contemplatively. In addition the steps that the mind takes quite impulsively must be recognized and then observed. Only then can we put a stop to this automatic process. The limiting of sensory contacts, as the Buddha explains it to us, presupposes that we stop constantly seeking out new things.

We know this kind of proliferation from nature. There are thousands of different species of flowers, plants, trees, and animals; and we heighten this by constantly adding new mixes and hybrids. Since this reproduction is part of nature, and as human beings we too are part of nature, we have the same drive toward proliferation. We want to experience as much as possible through our senses, and of course we also want to think a great deal about ever newer and more exciting things. In meditation we get a chance to practice not thinking, and even if we succeed only approximately, we shall find a little rest.

Because of the proliferation of natural and man-made things the supply of material for our senses is gigantic. Take, for example, the enticing array of products in the store windows. Nothing forces us to look at everything displayed there. It's quite clear that all these things are laid out only to awaken desires. And that happens in a flash. We glance at something that releases a pleasant feeling because it's pretty. At once the wish to possess is there, and if we can't have the thing in question because it's too expensive, the result will be disappointment and sadness. We can easily spare ourselves this range of feelings by just not looking. By limiting sensory contact we escape the constant need to have.

If we wish to meditate, in fact even before we begin to meditate, we are forced to limit our thinking. We do this by becoming mindful and consciously observing how we move and how we carry out our activities. We then extend this mindfulness to our thoughts.

In Western society, thinking a great deal has always been extolled. Philosophers were and are respected and famous individuals. Meanwhile none of them ever attained the goal of his thinking, and in many cases their ventures came to an unpleasant end because they had pondered far too much. This is proliferation in the mind. If we look upon thinking as the sixth sense, it becomes clear that it's just another gateway to the world. In meditation we have to shut that door, because during this time we don't want to have the world with us. We'll succeed in this only if we summon patience and perseverance, because the chatter in our heads can last for an unbelievably long time.

Here too, help is at hand. We observe our thoughts and stick a label on them. At that moment we become objective witnesses and stop being thinkers. Of course, thinking is a necessary part of everyday life. We can't write a letter, make a phone call, or carry on a conversation without thinking. That's why thinking has become such an inveterate habit that we can't drop it even when it gets in the way, as it does in meditation. In everyday life we find plenty of opportunities to practice not thinking. On a walk there is nothing to think about; one just looks or moves along. Isn't that enough? If we take the trouble to see, without thinking over what we have seen, we will quickly notice how difficult that is. But once we manage to do this, it's quite astonishing how it feels. You get a sense of great relief, a sense of floating without the weight of thinking. Thinking is suffering—like everything that moves. Thinking is movement, and movement creates friction, and friction is painful.

Naturally we can't survive without thinking. That's a fact. But since survival is by definition a losing battle, we have to set a different goal, something not so unreachable.

If we realize that the sixth sense—thinking—is the one that gives us the most trouble, we can lessen our pain by learning to bring the mind—thinking—to rest as often as possible.

It's same with hearing as with seeing. As soon as we hear something, either a pleasant or an unpleasant sensation arises. We name it and then react to it, with affection or rejection. If we succeed in not assigning any valuation to the sound, there will be no thought process.

Let's imagine that someone is beginning to swear at us in a booming voice. What's happening here? Nothing much, it's only a loud noise. There's no real reason, not the slightest, for reacting. It won't become anything more than a noise until we give in to the feeling and react. The reaction to being cursed will likely turn out to be negative. That's how most of the unpleasantness in life comes about. Seeing, smelling, tasting, and touching do not, for the most part, excite us as much as the things we hear. Only when these contacts are especially unpleasant will they provoke great excitement.

Thoughts trigger feelings. If we just think about something long enough, feelings will arise. This means that we have to guard and protect our mind. Just as thoughts are expressions of the mind, so are feelings. Unless we get a grip on this, we can't put our life on the harmonious foundation that we all want. We can't avoid all external occasions—there are too many of them. There are too many people who recognize or love us. There are numerous situations that we can't make friends with, and there's always the possibility that things will work out badly for us.

Only one thing is important here: to look inside ourselves. If only we ourselves were good, we could assume that the world around us would appear good too. But that's probably a fantasy. Still, if we change within and take a different perspective, things will also look different outside. If we look through a telescope, for example, we get a different perspective than if we only use the naked eye. What we see, admittedly, is the same, but it looks different.

If we wish to guard and protect ourselves, then we have to begin with our thoughts. The Buddha calls this protection "the four great efforts." They are very important. We have to be familiar with them, recall them, and practice them. This means that the information must be there; and then we have to notice it, which is quite hard in itself, because most people are very forgetful. Finally we also have to apply these four great efforts.

Once we have done that, we have entered upon the spiritual path. It's actually quite simple and not even time-consuming, because we are occupied with thinking anyway.

The Four Great Efforts

When unwholesome thoughts have not yet arisen, do not let them arise.
When unwholesome thoughts have already arisen, do not let them go any further.
Let wholesome thoughts that have not yet arisen arise.
Take wholesome thoughts that have already arisen and carry them further.

Through meditation we learn that we don't have to believe our thoughts, because most of them are useless—especially during meditation, where they only get in the way—unless we gain some insight through them. Thus if we realize that thoughts are only thoughts, then we can classify them as wholesome or unwholesome, positive or negative. There's no need here for blame or pangs of conscience, only understanding. Just as in meditation we replace thoughts with breathing, in everyday life we replace unwholesome ideas with wholesome ones. This won't always work, but the more we practice, the simpler it gets.

The first step is the hardest: not even letting an unwholesome thought arise. We can recognize an unwholesome thought by the feeling that precedes it. If we note a sense of obscurity, heaviness, sadness, unhappiness, or discontent, an unwholesome thought will follow, with a whole series of negative effects in its wake. This negativity plays out in the mind and brings with it not just resistance and rejection, but hatred as well. Unwholesome thoughts arise because there is hatred in us. I would compare this to a jack-in-the-box. When one touches the lid, the puppet springs out. But if the puppet is removed, you can hammer on the lid all you want: nothing will jump out.

We try to justify our hatred by shifting the blame onto the one who triggers it—as a rule some other person. "What nerve he had! When someone provokes me like that, I see red! I really don't have to put up with that!" That's more or less how our rationalizations go. Meanwhile all harmful thoughts simply arise from the fact that hate exists at all. Naturally all people make mistakes, including ourselves. But is that a justification for hatred?

In the Buddha's cosmology there are thirty-one levels of existence. The human level is the fifth from the bottom. What is to be expected here? We must simply realize that it's pointless to be forever searching for the guilty party. There are billions of men and women on this earth, so it's not hard to find a few guilty ones. But we mustn't forget that the only person whom we can purify, the only one we can do anything about, is ourselves. That's why it's so important to deliberately develop our mindfulness. The point is to discover negative thoughts even as they are popping up in us. Recognize, no blame, change! Hate is easy to recognize: it hurts.

When we feel an unwholesome thought emerging, it will eventually be possible, by means of premonitions and strong mindfulness, to replace it with a wholesome thought even before it is formulated. This is quite learnable, but first we have to promote and develop inward mindfulness. If we didn't already have some mindfulness, we would be crushed the first time around.

Once we have discovered an unwholesome thought in us, we don't have to believe it. We simply have to recognize it: this is an unwholesome thought; it harms me because it doesn't make me happy, it disturbs me and makes my life more difficult.

Thoughts based on hatred are easy to recognize because they feel terrible. Everyone has been annoyed at some point and knows exactly how this feels. The same is true of hating someone. It feels as if we were thrusting arrows into our own heart. When we observe that, sooner or later we will notice that we are fools to hurt ourselves. People who sense a lot of hatred in themselves are much readier to practice, because they want to get rid of all that unpleasantness.

Craving is much harder to recognize, because it doesn't hurt. Often enough one gets what one wants, especially in such an affluent society as ours. Besides, craving produces a certain pleasure. So it's understandable that humans afflicted with craving aren't that willing to practice. They aren't that intent on obtaining insight into their heart. Because hatred is so painful and unpleasant, it's a better foundation for the practice of purification than craving.

But just the same, greed causes suffering, because what we long for isn't there. It has to be sought, and the desire to have it provokes inner discontent. This discontent must be acknowledged. If we are fully content for only five minutes in a row, we will know the difference. Contentment is a feeling of steadiness, as if we were resting securely on a rock where the surf can't touch us. Everybody knows what it's like to be discontented. We can trace back all our desires to the fact that we aren't fully content, because we desire more and better things. And since we don't get them, we are ruled by a feeling of inner emptiness.

The Buddha calls unfulfillment and discontent *dukkha* (Skt. *duhkha*). The word is very hard to translate, because it implies so much: unfulfillment, discontent, inner emptiness, pain, grief, tragedy, and pain are all part of it.

If we want to recognize greed or desire, we have to begin with discontent. If we aren't fully content—and hardly anyone is—we will be governed by the wish for something or other. Whatever we long for is tainted with craving. If we get it, we are satisfied for the moment. But then fear immediately arises: Can I keep it? And immediately thereafter we feel anger and hatred, if we can't keep whatever it is, if it is taken away from us, or if it breaks down. These feelings rule us from birth until death, and we wonder why we're not completely content and happy. We believe this is due to something that comes to us from outside. But discontent can reside only in one's own heart. Then perhaps we realize that what we're really looking for can't be found in the world at all, that it might be found in the spiritual realm—and already we have a new wish on our hands. But that wish won't be completely fulfilled until we pursue it with decisiveness and perseverance. Still, at least the wish for something higher has manifested itself; it's no longer desire for something lower.

If we already have a wholesome thought within us, we should carry it further. If we don't yet have it, we should awaken it in ourselves. We don't have to accept our thoughts as they are; we can always check their contents. This is the fourth foundation of mindfulness. The first is the body, the second is feeling, the third is our moods, and the fourth is the content of our thoughts. It's the content of our thoughts that makes us happy or unhappy. So there is scarcely anything more important than being mindful and continuously aware that one is a fool, that one makes oneself unhappy.

The Buddha, it is true, didn't call us fools, but he did call us children. Interestingly, in Pali the same word is used for both. He compared us to children who are so foolish that they go on playing in a house that's on fire; they don't have enough sense to drop their toys and run out. The burning house stands for the wheel of life and death, and the toys mean everything that we cling to: our body, our mind, people we love, our homes, cars, and possessions that we don't want to let go of. We think we have to hold on to all this because it belongs to us.

But does our body belong to us? Why then does it hurt us from time to time? Why does it die at the wrong moment? If it really belonged to us, we'd be able to have some sort of influence on it. And if not even our own body belongs to us, how can anything at all belong to us? Everything is in motion and passes away, even the earth and the universe. To get free from the problems of human life, we have to make the transition from an individual to a universal perspective. That can't be managed overnight, but the Buddha's guidelines lead in that direction. He shows us how our thoughts work, and how we can deal with them.

We believe in what we think, without examining whether it's beneficial or destructive, whether it makes us happy or unhappy. But we don't have to play along with this game. We can drop out of it by paying attention to our thoughts. We can give our mind the possibility of removing itself, every now and then, from the everyday world. The body can't do that, it's bound to the earth by gravity; but the mind isn't. We can deliberately keep turning our mind to what's healthful; then it can become mobile and expand. It will begin to experience what lies all around it, including the things that aren't visible to the eye. There is, after all, more in the world than what we can see with our eyes. The human senses are limited. We aren't yet able to see ultraviolet light, but bees can. We can't hear very high-pitched sounds, but dogs can. Even though we know this, we believe totally and completely in the impressions of our senses.

If our mind is free from unwholesome thoughts, it acquires the capacity to move out lightly and with élan above the weight of the everyday world. It can turn to what gives it happiness and peace, because it has learned to take a universal perspective. So we have to begin to set the mind free from what is destructive. That's the only protection we can give it; and meditation is the only way we can learn that. In meditation we learn not to react to all our feelings and sense impressions. With it we have a foundation for everyday life. This doesn't mean that we become indifferent. We acquire equanimity, which is something else entirely. Equanimity is based on understanding. Indifference, by contrast, is a false defense; it builds a wall so we can't be attacked. Indifference contains neither love nor sympathy, while equanimity connects with others and provokes no mood shifts. Everything is recognized as coming into existence and again passing away.

So if we limit our sensory contacts and guard our thoughts, that will help us to an inner peace that someday will be unshakable. This unshakable peace leads finally to absolute truth.

4. THE SIXTH FRUIT
Mindfulness and Clear Comprehension

THE FOUR POINTS OF CLEAR COMPREHENSION

Mindfulness of the Body

NEXT THE BUDDHA EXPLAINS to King Ajātasattu mindfulness and clear comprehension. The Buddha continually mentions the latter in connection with mindfulness. Mindfulness means being alert and observant; clear comprehension, on the other hand, means that we also recognize what we are being mindful of. It has a broader context than mindfulness. Clear comprehension can be described as an "explanation of understanding." Here there are four points to be noted and remembered, which will protect us from many dangers.

First, there is the reflection: What is the purpose of what I'm thinking and the intention behind it? If we deal consciously with this question, then there is a chance to simply let some things drop and so gain a lot of time and energy that we can put to better use elsewhere. Our life can't change until our thinking has changed. If we keep posing the question to ourselves "Why do I actually think that?" we'll track down the underlying causes. We think, for the most part, because we are used to it. Quite unconsciously our hatred and our desire, but also our love and compassion, find expression in our thoughts. So this first step serves to determine what's going on in our thoughts at the moment. The knowledge that thinking is a habit gives us the possibility of change. Part of this is recognizing the purpose of each particular thought and deciding whether that purpose is worth following up.

The next step should lead us to the question of whether we have the proper resources to turn into reality a thought that we have recognized as wholesome. This means, first of all, slowing down our reactions. That would be a true blessing, because most of our mistakes come from not allowing ourselves enough time for reflection; instead we speak and act impulsively. Most people have both pleasant and unpleasant experiences in their lives, with the one more or less balancing out the other. But these experiences are supposed to teach us not to keep making the same mistakes. If we give ourselves time to deliberate and compare, we can spare ourselves the frustration of repeated wrong decisions.

The next step of clear comprehension has to do with dhamma. The question of whether what we intend to do, and the means we plan to use to do it, are meaningful, is followed by this one: Are our intentions and the means we propose to use appropriate for the spiritual path? Egocentric thinking and action generally meet with no success or only limited success, because other people are just as self-centered as we are—which is what causes interpersonal problems. If, by contrast, we're talking about something helpful, where we are giving instead of receiving, where we show love instead of hatred and desire, then we can devote ourselves completely to it. In order to do that, we need more time and reflection than we would for impulsive and instinctive thinking. Instinct is always oriented to ego confirmation. But if we sense the possibilities of the dhamma teaching, which aims at renunciation, we'll need time to reflect and confirm that what we're thinking and doing is also aimed at spiritual growth. We can spare ourselves many disappointments this way.

So to begin with we raise the question: What's my purpose here? Then: Do I have the means to achieve this purpose? And third: Is all this in line with the dhamma? Both the end and the means have to be in line with the dhamma, because the end doesn't automatically justify the means. Acting in the spiritual sense means heeding our conscience.

We frequently, and all too gladly, ignore our conscience, because it's uncomfortable. But we can follow the voice of our conscience as a guideline; then we'll be thinking and acting truthfully and from the heart.

The fourth step serves as a kind of exit interview. Have we achieved the purpose we had intended? If not, why not? What went wrong? Were the means badly chosen? Was the goal perhaps not right from the very start? And if we were successful, then the questions are: Have I grown from this? Have I let go of anything? Were the end and the means in order, and was the achievement a blessing? These questions are profitable not only when we have to make major decisions. They are just as valuable in everyday life. But unfortunately all knowledge about what we should observe leads, all too often, to a false valuation of the capacities we have already acquired. We know about our obligation to be helpful, to let go of the ego, not to seek self-confirmation, not to be greedy, and not to hate. We know about love, which we should give to one and all. But what does this knowledge do for us without action? Precious little.

Knowledge must always be followed by practice. This readiness to keep practicing is the only thing that provides our life with a spiritual foundation. We ourselves can be our best teacher if we acknowledge our own mistaken attitudes. Only when the view is directed inward do we gradually get a picture of what's actually going on there. This gives us the capacity for spiritual growth. Often enough we'll recognize hatred, but chiding ourselves for that would be pointless. The hatred is there—just as the love is there. So blaming ourselves or regretting is the wrong kind of attitude. What matters is to understand and to keep on practicing. When a small child is learning to run, it constantly falls down, gets up and tries again, until one day it can run without difficulties. We too will keep getting up again and keep practicing further. We owe this to our capacity to love ourselves; because only if we show this patience and love for ourselves can we do it for others.

We have to accept the fact that we think we're the center of the universe. Of course, outside of us there are billions of people, each of whom feels that he or she is the center. If this center is not in order, how can the rest of the world be in order? Clear comprehension is a good guideline, because it plainly shows whether we have turned our knowledge into reality. We have to explore first the goal, then the means for reaching the goal; next, whether both do justice to dhamma, and finally the result.

If we busy ourselves enough with these four points, such reflections will finally become a habit, because the mind is subject to its habits.

The Buddha often calls this clarity of comprehension the companion of mindfulness. Mindfulness (*sati*) and clear comprehension (*sampajañña*) are usually mentioned together. With mindfulness we have to keep an eye not just on ourselves, but also on what's happening in the world around us. In any event mindfulness is never bound up with judging, much less with condemning—it is merely recognizing.

The first field of practice for mindfulness is the body. Here breathing plays a crucial role for meditative rest. All other domains of mindfulness of the body are oriented to understanding. But when we observe during breathing, we can also note its coming into being and passing away. If our mind is particularly stubborn and refuses to concentrate, then we should direct it to the coming and going of breath. Then we can get to know the arising and ceasing of everything else that we are made of, such as thoughts, feelings, and all bodily functions. From this we can gain the deep insight that everything moves. The more we direct our attention to this impermanence, the closer we come to the truth.

Mindfulness of breathing teaches us one more extraordinarily important lesson. Although we can control it for a short time, it's there even if "I" don't do anything. The body breathes, from which we can conclude whether or not an "I" may be found anywhere in the body.

If we observe the movements of the body, we can also get a very good view of arising and ceasing. It's simply impossible for a bodily movement to be permanent. It has happened, and it has to come to an end to make way for a new one. Otherwise we would turn into pillars of salt.

Everything that we know, think, or see is a relative truth. Of course there are individual beings with names and features. Each one has at his or her disposal identification signs such as man/woman, young/old, ugly/pretty, and so forth. But these are mere conventional labels. All these classifications arise, change, and pass away. And that is an absolute truth. Mindfulness must aim at recognizing that everything which comes into being passes away. With each of our movements it's clear that the mind has commanded them. The mind says: The bell just rang, go to the door. Or: Watch out, be careful. We obey. Meanwhile, where does the "me" reside? Is the "me" the mind that gives the order, or is it the body that carries it out? This thought will shake up our understanding of what we previously took for granted, which is itself a great gain. Only in this way can we eventually move from relativity to universality, from relative truth to absolute truth.

We have now observed breath and bodily movement in their impermanence. Besides these, the Buddha mentions the four bodily postures: sitting, walking, standing up, and lying down.

Arising and ceasing apply to all functions, but in bodily postures we can notice one more thing: restlessness. Our body never leaves us quite content, and hence the mind reacts with unrest. When we have lain down for a long time, we want to get up; when we have stood up, we want to lie down. The nature of the mind is restless too and always seeking change. This is an expression of our discontent, which only the fully enlightened person can escape. For us, however, it's crucial to recognize that restlessness is our nature. Once we have recognized and accepted this, we needn't follow every suggestion of the mind. If we've ceased to be slaves of this restlessness, we can decide whether to give in to it or, if at the moment we consider it appropriate, to resist. Thus we have gained an important insight. Everyone who makes an honest effort can profit from the Buddha's explanation. Even meditating while out on a walk creates an opportunity for the mind to come to rest, because in the process one concentrates on the movement of walking. Here too we can observe arising and ceasing. Anyone who asks himself or herself while walking: "So where is the 'me,' where is the 'me' during this walk?" has made an attempt to find out the truth. It doesn't have to be successful; simply trying is enough.

Some people can't reach understanding until they've found rest in meditation. Here too there are different methods that can help us. One of them is investigating the different parts of the body. The Buddha speaks of the thirty-two parts of the body. We could learn these by heart, but generally that's not necessary, because everyone knows his or her anatomy well enough. We could imagine opening our bodies with a zipper, taking out the individual parts—gallbladder, liver, kidneys, blood vessels, sinews, intestines, lungs, heart—and laying them out in front of us. We observe mindfully which part might contain the "me." We'll never find it. We won't find anything pretty, because the organs are purely functional, not pretty. Now that we have taken everything out and it's lying in front of us, we go about removing the bones and laying them down. There's still no "me" in sight. The only thing left now is shriveled-up skin—not likely that the "me" is hidden in there. After we've carefully searched, we put the body back together again, close the zipper, and suddenly there it is again: "me." If we now find ourselves breathing a sigh of relief, we know that we are still very much identified with our body.

With this insight into our own body we gain some distance from our strong body-identification. Although many people claim they would never believe that the "me" is in their body, they are nonetheless full of body-related desires and longings. Here too we have a spiritual error. Once you have tried this exercise of pulling yourself apart, you'll think a little bit differently about yourself.

Yet another method of obtaining insight is contemplating the four basic elements from which all material things are made. First comes the element of earth—solid things—our flesh and bones, hair, nails, teeth. The element of fire is body temperature. More than seventy percent of us is the element of water, which holds us together. If we take flour and add water we get dough, because water binds it together. What we recognize in ourselves as the element of water are blood, saliva, urine, tears, sweat. If it weren't for the intercellular fluid, our cells wouldn't hold to-gether. Just imagine them wandering all over the place. That might even help us to call our self-centeredness into question, but in the final analysis we would probably label the largest cell "me" anyway. The fourth element is wind or air. This is made up, naturally, of the breath and the winds of the body; part of this is movement too, because wind is always moving and air is dis-placed by movement.

These are the four primary elements of the universe, of which all material things are composed. If we deal meditatively with the elements, we can determine that our whole environment con-sists of the same basic elements. Take the floor, for example: it's solid, has a temperature, holds together, and so must have the water element in it. If it didn't, the floor would consist of noth-ing but tiny separate particles without any bond between them. Further, there is constant motion, which is why things fall apart. Nothing exists that doesn't fall apart; hence everything moves. Unfortunately we can't see this with our bodily eye, otherwise things would be much simpler. In meditation, however, this process can be observed with the mind's eye; and it's obvious that it couldn't be any other way. It's important to come to realize that everything—including ourselves—consists of these ele-ments.

It's also interesting that every individual element contains all the others. Thus, for example, water also has a solid element of earth, otherwise no boat could sail over it and no fish could swim in it. It also has temperature and, as we know, movement. The same is true of the element of air. If it didn't have something solid in it, no bird or plane could stay aloft. Thus the four ele-ments are contained, in various quantities, in human beings. If we judged by our physical sensations, we would be inclined to ascribe the largest share in us to the element of earth. But that isn't true, since we already know that we consist mostly of water. We can't see or feel that; but in meditation, when with increased mindfulness we journey into ourselves, we begin to recognize that there isn't much to the compactness we believe so devoutly in. We can readily perceive the constant motion that prevails in us. Movement is the nature of our body. We begin to suspect that solidity is just an illusion that spreads a veil over coming into existence and passing away. Examining the four elements in contemplation has nothing to do with discursive thinking or intellectual comprehension. It is a voyaging into ourselves, and a holding before one's eyes the fact that everything in existence is made up of the same four elements, and hence that we're connected with everything. It's particularly helpful to recall that all humans are made of the same matter—with the minor detail that this matter is put together somewhat differently from one case to the next, and so varies in appearance.

Knowledge of our connectedness with everything that's alive helps to allay our existential anxiety somewhat. Even feelings of hatred are diminished this way; and so this method is a further step toward insight and truth, and helps us to reach a more restful and serene life. So long as the mind hasn't yet become peaceful in meditation, it's necessary, first of all, to acquire understanding. Once the mind has come to rest, understanding can be considerably strengthened in meditation. Only profound rest makes it possible to have penetrating insights that open up altogether new perspectives. Still, every step brings us somewhat closer to this ideal.

The next practice in mindfulness of the body is observing. First of all, there is observing the body through contemplation. The Buddha called this "looking at the field of corpses," because it teaches us that we are exposed to sickness, decay, and death. That expression comes from the fact that in the Buddha's time, and even today, corpses were laid out on the cremation sites and could be seen by everyone.

Hence, in this contemplation we should look upon ourselves as corpses—and not just as a dead body, but as everything that goes along with it. We should try to experience our death. On this point the Buddha gave different versions of this meditation. We are to see ourselves as a skeleton, perhaps even as scattered bones, or as a recently deceased body, which is already swollen, discolored, and being eaten by worms.

In this context the Buddha has been criticized for describing only negative things, but the truth is quite different. The Buddha's teachings are about the Middle Way. Since we all strongly identify with our body and don't want to lose it, we have to experience how things really are. The Buddha's methods aim to bring us there, because one day we will lie dead. This is a fact that we can't get around, much as we would like to.

We should visualize it daily. When we have overcome this inner resistance, our attitude to life will change. Not until one has given one's life, can it really be experienced as it is. This is a turning to the truth and to the realization that all our wishing and striving, all the stress from hatred and rejection, all our many desires are quite unnecessary. Where does the path lead? Always and without exception back to the earth, to dust and ashes. Everybody knows this, and nobody believes it; no one lives in accordance with the truth. All the efforts of human beings are directed at security and long duration. This is absurd, because such things don't exist and never will. We have to recognize how fleeting the body is. It might be gone tomorrow, or even tonight—if that should happen. And who will finish all the things I've started? In any case it would be better to leave nothing unfinished.

Once we have managed to visualize our body in various stages of decay, we can imagine the moment of death. Surely everyone has enough imagination for that. Perhaps something will emerge all by itself in contemplation if we have already looked into these ideas. Most likely the mind won't be especially eager for this and will turn away. Then we'll have to patiently repeat the whole process as long as necessary until we accept it. This is the truth—this is what it looks like.

But we don't have to be just inwardly wakeful. Here there are two major points: What's the reason, what came over me from the outside, that I'm now reacting in this way? Why am I startled? Why do I clench my teeth? Why do I shrug my shoulders? It's important that we don't continue to act impulsively, but become conscious that we are reacting and how we are reacting. All the factors are discernible, but being mindful will make it easier for us to change something or let it go.

The second kind of mindfulness is "looking outward" at what is happening physically. That would refer, first of all, to the elements within us, which likewise exist all around us. Contemplating this helps us to feel connected with everything that lives. Once we've recognized this sameness, a feeling of belonging will arise that gives us security.

In exactly the same way we can observe other people mindfully. We'll notice how they move, for example, and we can decide whether we wish to physically express ourselves in that way or another. Here it's vital not to judge—and certainly not to condemn. Other persons are simply to serve as a mirror, because we're quite blind when we observe ourselves. Perhaps we realize that we ourselves could be much more mindful. The world around us is nothing but a mirror image of ourselves.

Hence the saying that only a Buddha recognizes a Buddha. That is, we can't imagine anything that we haven't already experienced. How should we recognize an Enlightened One, when we have no idea what an Enlightened One is like? By contrast, we recognize an angry person immediately, because we ourselves have been angry often enough. Everything that we know about others is what we bear within ourselves. What we reject in others, we repress in ourselves. We simply don't admit that we have exactly the same unpleasant side. So we should beware condemning others, because in so doing we are actually condemning ourselves. We should use this mirror-image function to direct more mindfulness to our own thinking and action. Without condemnation. Only to recognize.

If we keep turning our mindfulness inward, we'll achieve clarity about our reactions. The more difficult a situation is, the more we can learn from it. There's no better lesson than an emergency. We should be grateful for the blows of fate, because nothing else enables us to make such good progress. Have we become so mindful that we ask: "What should I learn from this event? What's it all about? How come I have such a hard time coping with precisely this sort of situation?" Then we've learned a great deal, and we'll find it easier to deal with everyone.

5. THE SIXTH FRUIT
Mindfulness of Feeling, Mind, and Mental Objects

THREE FACTORS OF ENLIGHTENMENT

THE SECOND FOUNDATION of mindfulness is feeling. We believe that we love from the mind—but it isn't true. Our thinking is only a reaction to feelings. Our emotions press all the buttons for our behavior. We think the way our feeling has dictated: Pleasant—I want it. Unpleasant—I reject it. Thus we are constantly reacting to our feelings. Unless we see through this it will keep on going the same way. The way out of this cycle is mindfulness, which gives us insights into our interior life.

Our reactions are always the same: desires, which also include rejections. Here it's a question of the first and second of the Four Noble Truths that make up the essence of the Buddha's teaching. At the moment of his enlightenment the Buddha formulated these Four Noble Truths. The first states that dukkha—suffering, unfulfillment, and discontent—exists. The second Noble Truth is that there is only one reason for this: craving—wanting and not wanting. We can easily discern this in ourselves. Once we have done so, two things happen. First, it brings us closer to the Buddha's teaching, and second, we come to trust. Without that we have no basis for practice; we remain constantly preoccupied with ourselves and our opinions.

If we let the Buddha's teachings work on us, we'll realize how to get rid of dukkha—namely, by simply letting go of craving, of desire. It's true, "simply" isn't quite accurate, but we have to keep practicing letting go on a small scale. If we vehemently wish for something and are convinced that we deserve it, but still have difficulties in getting it because someone else is competing with us, then we have a problem. We'll get rid of it only when we let go of wanting. Once we sense the relief that this behavior brings us, we'll keep practicing it. That way letting go gets easier. If we consider what has become obvious after looking at the field of corpses, then we know that we can't take anything into the grave anyway. Whether it's emotions or material things, we can't take it with us. Letting go of desires is the lever that releases an inner sense of being unburdened.

Hence there are two things that must be done to help us to inner harmony. First, examine our feelings before we react to them. If we sense anger, rejection, desire, or pain, we shouldn't react immediately, but should check to see what it's really about. Hatred, for example, can be unleashed through bodily sensations. When we sit in meditation and our leg begins to hurt, the feeling of rejection is there at once, along with the reaction: "I don't want this." But we can meet it by realizing that even though we can react, we don't have to.

So long as we blindly react to our feelings, we have no choice. We won't get a sense of freedom until we've learned to test the feelings and to let them go. If we learn in meditation not to move our leg until we want to, we're making a choice. And we can carry this over to our everyday life. If we've recognized that people have pleasant and unpleasant emotions, and that the way out of this is not to react, that will make it easier to apply this knowledge and practice letting go.

We shouldn't think that we have a birthright to enjoy pleasant feelings and nothing else. This is a widespread error in affluent societies. Unpleasant feelings are part of us too. So we have to keep directing mindfulness inward, to our feelings, with the question: What caused this feeling? If we notice the feeling in others, we can accept it as a mirror-image function, because we've felt it often enough ourselves and can resolve not to react that way anymore. But trying to hand out advice to another person at such a time is useless. We must know that a person whose mind has been clouded by feelings is in no position to listen. Feelings are part of the mind too.

Beyond that, we can fathom our own mental attitude, which

is initially perceived as nothing but a mood. Now we have to ascertain whether it is leaning more toward consent or rejection, more positive or negative. Our mindfulness can be compared to a microscope: with its help we can see much more clearly what is going on in our laboratory. That way we gain a more objective view of ourselves and a little more distance from the subjective "It happened to me," "I have to do that," "The world is against me." This "me," "mine," and "I" are called into question when we examine ourselves closely. Of course, we'll still notice what's going on in other people, but that knowledge should never result in blame; it should only be a mirror image. The more we make use of it, the more comprehensive our overview will be. In a large mirror we recognize exactly what we ourselves and others look like.

The third foundation of mindfulness is our mental state. Mental states include everything that arises, whether anger or upset, anxiety or fear, ease or tension. The mind may be malleable and quiet, or restless and worried. If we want to know ourselves intimately, we have to be mindful enough to recognize our states of mind and also realize that we are only reacting to a pleasant, unpleasant, or neutral feeling. These in turn come about automatically due to our sense contacts.

Sense contacts that create feelings can be easily ascertained. If two people apply for the same job and one is ugly and the other one good-looking, it is quite likely that the person in charge may choose the good-looking one. He or she would, in that case, be swayed by pleasant feelings without any rationale or logic about it. People applying for a job usually put on good clothes and make sure they look attractive. Why would they do that? They want to make a good impression, which in turn creates a pleasant feeling, followed by a favorable perception, which achieves the desired reaction of being accepted.

We need to know and watch our mental states, because the negative ones pollute our mind. Most of humanity is more than half the time angry or upset, disappointed, or restless, and because of that, the world is in a state of constant turmoil.

The only way we can bring happiness to ourselves and to those around us, and at the same time contribute toward peace, is to recognize our own negative states—not blame ourselves, but change. This is the work of a mindful practitioner and will change our lives and those around us, even if we do not catch our negativities every time. The people we live and work with will have the benefit of a positive and supportive mind state, which they can rely upon, relax into, and emulate. If we want to be a dedicated dhamma practitioner, we have to become an example to others in everyday life.

An important aspect of this is learned in meditation. When discursive thinking interrupts us and we label that, we have already learned to look inside ourselves, to realize when we are irritated, rejecting, resisting, angry, worried, or disappointed. Having practiced to replace our discursive thinking with attention on the breath again and again, we can do exactly the same in daily life. In that way our meditation bears immediate fruit. One day we may not need to substitute unwholesome mind states anymore, because they have stopped arising. But as long as they still plague us, we need to let go of them. Substitution is a most effective way of dealing with that.

The same unwholesome mental state may have to be conquered more than once. The formula is "Recognize, no blame, change"—even if that has to be done over and over again. Most people believe that their negativities arise because others have initiated them. If we think outside triggers are to blame, we have no chance to pursue our inner happiness. Often we find fault with the person closest to us at home or at work. If we do not see the absurdity of that, we have meditated in vain.

Our speech and actions arise out of our mental states. No other cause can be found for them. Therefore our mind states are of the utmost importance for our well-being and harmonious living. Our first line of defense against unhappiness is refusing to believe that we are the victims of the bad intentions of others. The formula is: Do not blame the trigger. The world is full of triggers; in fact, life is designed like that, so that we will truly practice. We can be grateful for all these triggers, as without them we might never recognize our own unfortunate reactions.

We have a built-in capacity for dislike, but we equally have an inherent faculty of love. For some absurd reason, we seem to prefer dislike and ill will to our potential for love. If we were to practice love and compassion, we would live in a different world, and also our mass media would be filled with totally different contents. The reason for this absurdity is that loving consists in giving and therefore letting go of self-cherishing, which is never easy to do. Dislike, however, is based on hate, and we are proud of our discriminatory abilities, so that rejection is closer to the surface out of habit and self-endorsement. But all of us have the ability to reverse this trend.

Bare and pinpointed attention will also help us to realize that negative mental states again act as triggers for unpleasant feelings. In this way, it will become clear that we are experiencing the same inner conditions over and over again. One could use the simile of being preprogrammed. If we want benefit from meditation and a harmonious and peaceful life, we must learn to take our attention off one object and place it on another one when needed. Here meditation and daily life require the same mental action. As we become more and more aware of ourselves, we will realize that we only know that on which our attention is focused. If we do not use our mind for what it is really intended, we are wasting a good human life, which is an unfortunate but common occurrence. The real purpose of human consciousness is purification, which brings great and lasting benefit to us now and in the future. Everyone having contact with a purified mind experiences well-being and happiness, so that the results are far-reaching.

When mindfulness becomes clear and pinpointed enough to recognize our mental states, we will also realize the results we are experiencing. Negative states of mind are invariably followed by unpleasant feelings, which should tell us quite clearly that these mental states are not useful. But instead of seeing how they have arisen, we usually look for a scapegoat, which then culminates in disliking a certain person. Naturally this results in more unpleasant feelings, and we are again caught in our preprogrammed reactions. Hopefully we will see from this that we are producing our own unhappiness and nobody else is involved.

When we learn to dissect the mind into its four most prominent aspects, the *khandas*—sense contact, feeling, perception, and mental formation—we can then be aware of their functions without having to make that a personal statement. Our perceptions are imbued with our opinions and desires and can therefore never be totally reliable. But when we understand the four parts of mind operating as cause and effect, continuously repeating themselves, our perception of ourselves and the world around us changes. We begin to see ourselves as the process of four states of mind following each other, and a lot of greed and hate will then fall away, since this process does not really include a "me" and "myself." Because of that, there is more clarity in the mind, which brings different views to light. Enlightenment essentially means a clear and unobstructed mind that realizes through inner seeing. This kind of seeing does not happen with our physical eyes but through an inner vision. The Buddha uses the words "knowledge and vision of things as they really are." Our practice brings us to the understood experience, which utilizes knowing and seeing.

These four parts of mind are used by all of us constantly, day in, day out, decade after decade, lifetime after lifetime, from morning to night without interruption. Yet we have no inkling that we are preprogrammed and constantly reacting to either pleasant or unpleasant feelings. In fact, most of the time, we do not even know our feelings, just our reactions, which means we have the experience but no understanding of it.

The Buddha's teaching shows us a certain way of observing ourselves, and when we then have the same experience over and over again, we may recognize the significance of it. This is how wisdom arises. There is no substitute for the understood experience, which is true *vipassanā*, or insight. We might think of experiences as something exciting or special, but in reality they happen every moment. Our senses contact objects, and we react but do not consciously take notice. Consequently we get restless because we would like something more interesting to occur.

What could actually be more interesting than finding out about ourselves? We usually consider it stimulating to meet people, discuss all sorts of subjects, and find out what they think. Isn't it more important to find out what we ourselves are thinking? When we know ourselves, we will know what everybody else's mind is doing. The Buddha said, "The whole of the universe lies in this mind and body." Paying attention to ourselves is the essence of mindfulness.

In daily life many things distract us from being attentive to ourselves. Driving a car, walking across a busy street, writing a letter, answering the telephone. All these things need to be done and take one outside oneself. But having practiced mindfulness in meditation, our daily chores can also be done with attention to the smallest detail, so that the mind becomes more and more one-pointed.

How can we ever find out who we truly are if we do not inquire into our mind and its actions and reactions? If we understand intellectually that our usual perceptions of ourselves and the world are a mistaken view and never help to bring fulfillment into our hearts, this will help to put us on the path.

Mindfulness is the mental state that opens the door for us to greater understanding. When we use clear-cut, unembellished total awareness of what is actually happening, we need not think about the possible repercussions and explanations connected with the event. Mindfulness is knowing only, without interpretations. In order to practice, we need this kind of pinpointed attention to slow down. When we look at something or hear a sound, we remain focused on seeing or hearing. Then we can become aware of the sequence of events following the sense contact. Since the subsequent steps of feeling, perception, and reaction arise at such speed, we have to repeatedly direct our attention to the initial sense contact, so that we can notice the next step, which then also arises repeatedly. In that way we may recognize how we make our own world happening. The sequence is so quick that it ordinarily escapes us, primarily because we never thought it was important to pay attention.

Mindful objectivity toward our mental states is often sufficient to make them dissolve. It is the same as in meditation, when the naming of the discursive thoughts makes them fall apart. The one who is the observer does not remain the thinker or the victim. We cannot observe and be anxious, irritated, or upset at the same time. We receive great benefit right then and there, in less than a second.

This is something quite wonderful that everyone can do. The Buddha taught ordinary people like ourselves; and if he had thought they would be unable to follow his guidelines, he would have been wasting his time. All we need is some understanding of the fact that happiness is eluding us. If we did not know that we have dukkha, why would we want to meditate? We could spend our time with so many of the available distractions. Admitting a lack of fulfillment to oneself is a sign of being awake and aware. To deny one's own dukkha is an escape mechanism, which has a certain viability, but cannot work forever.

Besides practicing this mindful observation in everyday life, it is very useful to address it also in meditation, because when the mind is not totally concentrated, mental-emotional states keep arising. We notice them, name them, and replace them with the meditation object. The more we learn that in meditation, the more easily we can continue this habit in all situations. Formerly, we believed in those states and did not recognize the fact that they are strictly moods, which arise and cease. When we believe each thought that we have, we live according to its impact on us. We try to escape from what we believe to be the causes of our negative states and attach ourselves to what we believe to be the condition for our positive reactions. Since this effort is in vain and bound to be unsuccessful, we are never at ease, always searching for fulfillment. Finally we may come to the conclusion that it is up to us to change our mental-emotional states. That will be the opening of the spiritual path for us—a path that goes beyond meditation and includes mindfulness from morning to night.

The content of thoughts is the fourth foundation of mindfulness. When we use it as a purification process, we make not only meditation easier, but all of life as well. Of course, "good" and "bad" remain, but if we have acquired the capacity to stress the good in us, then we're also doing something for the world around us.

The contents of the mind can be shaped by the various parts of the Buddha's teaching: the five hindrances and the Four Noble Truths, the fourth of which, the Eightfold Path, can lead us to freedom. It's interesting to know that the first of the seven factors of enlightenment is mindfulness. Obviously it's the access to the spiritual foundation. It's the spice of life and prevents any kind of boredom. If you direct mindfulness to yourself, to your own thoughts and feelings, interest in spiritual growth always remains.

The second of the seven factors of enlightenment is the study of phenomena. The expression *dhamma* comes up in this context. As mentioned, *dhamma* means the teaching of the Buddha, but also truth and the law of nature. In addition *dhamma* is the word for "phenomenon." Everything that exists is dhamma. That means we need to pay objective attention to everything that exists. All phenomena should be tested with a view to their transitoriness, their inability to satisfy, and their insubstantiality. But this constant scrutiny won't become a factor of enlightenment until we've perfected it, and that has to be preceded by long, steady practice. Meanwhile we've observed the arising and ceasing of our movements, feelings, and thoughts. If we keep this knowledge clearly in our memory, then we're practicing the second factor of enlightenment—the examination of phenomena by mindfully observing their coming into existence and passing away.

Anicca (impermanence), *dukkha* (suffering), and *anattā* (nonself) have been called the three characteristic features of the universe. We should choose one of these characteristics and work with it until another engages us more, and then explore that one.

If we take the concept of dukkha, the following questions emerge: Does dukkha really exist everywhere and in everything, as the Buddha said? How can dukkha be in everything? Quite simply, because nothing remains as it is. Everything comes into existence and passes away. Nothing, not even the most pleasant thing, is absolutely satisfying, because we can't hold on to it. We haven't yet entered the river of arising and ceasing; we still want to cling to the shore. If for the moment someone has a lot of dukkha, it can be helpful to see whether there really is a universal dukkha or perhaps only a personal one. Those who have no dukkha just now won't be very interested in it, because they are thankful not to be suffering. But that's only superficial. If we go into the depths, we'll quickly notice that here too dukkha reigns. Again and again we keep coming back to dukkha, because dukkha and impermanence turn into one another and lead to the last feature, insubstantiality.

Nowhere can we discover anything that remains intact, nowhere is there solidity, a core we can hold on to. True, we all try to, but no one succeeds. And so no one is properly happy. The Buddha always warned against simply believing or rejecting what he said. Either would be foolish, he thought. We should see for ourselves whether it adds up.

People with a great deal of trust in the Buddha's teaching often choose impermanence as an object of investigation. Those with an analytical bent will more likely take on insubstantiality. A person who is good at concentrating will turn to dukkha as a theme. Sometimes we'll have an experience like the peeling of an onion: one layer after another is stripped away until in the end we're left with nothing at all. And yet the onion looked so solid— except that there was no core. Sooner or later constant testing leads us to take a much more realistic view of the world and ourselves. Enlightenment, freedom, and a lack of problems become a feeling that stays with us. Although these investigations are carried out with the mind, they help us to achieve inner change.

In meditation too we can observe arising and ceasing, which can lead to dukkha. Dukkha isn't just physical or emotional pain, but above all else the inner voice that tells us, "I'm not perfectly fulfilled; there must be something more than this. Where is it?" Then comes the moment when we no longer seek fulfillment outside ourselves, because we realize that the inner void is the real dukkha; and we can experience fullness only when we transcend the world. So long as we think that our dukkha comes from outside, there will be no spiritual path. Until we reach enlightenment, dukkha is a part of our existence.

In meditation we can also scrutinize insubstantiality by looking into ourselves and seeing if we can find a core substance that remains unchangeable. It's important to do this examination because only that way can we reach wisdom.

The third factor of enlightenment that can be helpful to us here is the intellectual energy that's bound up with willpower and self-discipline. When the mind keeps its eyes wide open and experiences things clearly, there's energy present. When the mind is clouded over or roams through the world, there is no willpower behind it; and this factor is missing. In serenity meditation (*samatha*) we automatically summon up mind-energy. We can compare this to the body: when we give the body no rest, it quickly runs out of gas. The mind needs the same thing. We must enable it to spiritualize itself, to rest, to take itself to a level of consciousness that has nothing to do with the everyday routine, and to wait there. This leads to a strong supply of fresh energy that's absolutely necessary in order to follow the spiritual path successfully.

The first three factors of enlightenment—mindfulness, examination of phenomena, and energy—are called mind objects, and with mindfulness we can tell whether any of them is present. With mindfulness we also know whether one of the Four Noble Truths is present in the mind, which refers particularly to the first two: namely, that we have dukkha, and that we have it because we either desire something or wish to get rid of something. This is a crucial realization. If we let go of desire even once, we have already taken a great step and can repeat it.

We always think that enlightenment is something for spiritual geniuses, something that exists off in the cloudy distance, with no connection to us. But at the end of his discourse on mindfulness the Buddha said what amounts to this: if you really practice mindfulness for seven years, you will undoubtedly come to the fruit of the non-returner (the almost-enlightened) or the Enlightened One. And he continues: "But no, not seven years, six years, five years, four years, three years, two years, one year. No, not even one year, eleven months, ten months . . . one month. No, not even that. If someone practices perfect mindfulness for seven days, he must without a doubt come to the fruit of the almost or fully enlightened person."

QUESTIONS AND ANSWERS

Q: What do Christians mean by "free will"? They can't possibly mean desire?

A: The Buddha means that we operate with free will in our sphere. One has to imagine a dog tied to a leash. This leash is our old kamma. The dog can move as far as the leash stretches. If he does only good things in his domain, then the leash gets longer and longer; more and more possibilities of doing good or evil come about. So we always have free will to choose good or evil. It's like the training of children. At first we have to tell toddlers everything, even how to go to the toilet. When they get bigger, we increasingly leave them more free will, because they're capable of taking responsibility for themselves. It's just the same with us.

Q: You say that with mindfulness there's no boredom. What happens to me is that for a while I find mindfulness quite beautiful, and I get better and better at it. But after I have been quite mindful for a time, I get terribly bored, and I take absolutely no pleasure in it. I assume that this condition will not change anytime soon. The question is whether it would be right, for the time being, to be mindful just for a certain period. Twenty-four hours is too much.

A: Twenty-four hours would include sleeping, but with sleeping it gets very hard. Being mindful during sleep is a very special gift and stage of development. True, the Buddha did it, but most people have no way to do it. Being mindful for sixteen hours a day is hard. I don't believe mindfulness is dropped deliberately; rather it's dropped because of the incapacity to go on. Then you bring out mindfulness again and continue on. That's how it is for everyone.

Mindfulness of Feeling, Mind, and Mental Objects | 87

Q: But then the stress continues longer than if you just tell yourself, O.K., now you don't have to be mindful anymore. If you keep dropping mindfulness and then have to pick it up again, a certain amount of stress is still there, which builds up toward the evening.

A: Toward evening the mind may get tired and want to surrender to its weariness. That's quite natural; then you have to give in to it in this respect. Mindfulness is an alert, observant mental attitude that's occupied with our inner life and with actions. Perhaps mindfulness is being experienced as an unwanted obligation, so that an internal protest is launched against it. That would be a worthwhile thing to find out.

Q: What's the motive force behind our action?

A: Willpower gets us cranked up. As long as we're not completely fulfilled, we will continue to have wishes. There is a parable on the subject of willpower. Two frogs have fallen into a pail of milk and can't get out. They thrash around to keep from drowning. Finally one frog says: "I can't do it anymore, I don't want to anymore!" But the other frog has decided: "I want to swim until my strength deserts me." In the end, his swimming and thrashing have turned the milk to butter. He finds himself on top of a mountain of butter and hops out of the pail.

6. THE SEVENTH AND EIGHTH FRUITS
Contentment and Patience

THE FIRST JHĀNA

AFTER THE BUDDHA has explained mindfulness in detail to Ajātasattu and presented it to him as a fruit of renunciation, the king is quite content. But he wants to know more. He thinks renunciation must produce other fruits too.

Mindfulness means renouncing the usual mind games and desires. When we are mindful, we can't desire something at the same time. In the same way, meditation is first of all a renunciation, a letting go of what we usually do with our mind. This renunciation will later bear rich fruit, but in the beginning we don't know this. For this reason the Buddha approves the question about the further fruits of renunciation and explains that contentment is a consequence of having no wishes. If, for example, we sit down to meditate and are completely without expectations, indifferent to how it will go, then we sense a feeling of happiness. But if we are at odds with ourselves, because our expectations weren't met, because we didn't find as much happiness as we had hoped for, then the mind becomes discontented as a result of the unfulfilled wishes. We have to earn contentment by taking things as they are. We can accomplish that only if we let go of our wishes. We can observe this in ourselves: as soon as a feeling of discontent shows up, there must be an unfulfilled wish somewhere.

The Buddha advised us to have patience. In meditation itself having patience with ourselves is indispensable. We have to patiently maintain our efforts at meditating, but we shouldn't expect anything, because expectations lead to disappointment.

Hence in daily life too we should give up expectations for ourselves and others. That's not so easy. Attitudes of expectation are generally tied in with excessive demands on ourselves and are based on personal pride: "I should have been able to do that. . . . But I know better. . . . I expect myself to be perfect." This personal pride produces constant unrest, which inevitably brings with it a whole series of problems. We and others are simply incapable of meeting excessive expectations. Instead, we should practice mindfulness and simply recognize what's there. When mindfulness is coupled with clear comprehension, then we can change something.

So we should develop patience in dealing with ourselves. We should give up the expectant attitude, since it always leads to disappointment, and practice mindfulness, because that's the only way to get to clear knowledge. In patience we see a letting go of ego assertion. When we're impatient, we want to shape things in line with our own intentions. Those who have patience can wait, and since everything is always changing, what's happening right now will change too. With patience everything can be easily borne; with impatience—which also means rejection—things are borne only with difficulty. This is of the utmost importance, especially in meditation. We should never reject our own meditation, regardless of how unfocused we may have been during it. We have to develop patience and contentment, so that we can practice. It's not the end of the journey that counts, but the journey itself. If we are intent only on getting to the goal quickly, we'll miss all the beauty en route; and in addition we become impatient and discontented over spending the time needed to reach the goal. We will never have a beautiful trip that way.

So what matters is the journey itself: every step inward is significant, regardless of whether it seems successful to us. The success we are waiting for is only an opinion that we've formed. Whether it's true is open to question. Every step, even the tiniest one, brings us further. And so, wishing for little gives contentment, and with patience we can ease the journey. It's useless to get all sorts of ideas about how things ought to be. The point is to recognize how they really are. Wishes for success and expectations conceal the results of the moment because we aren't even conscious that they're already there.

We want to find our way to rest, but we fail to, because we forget that we first have to take the steps to help us advance on the spiritual path. The first step is the intention to meditate. The Buddha says: "Intention is kamma." Our intentions create our kamma all by themselves. So if we sit down with the intention of concentrating, of just letting go of our thoughts in order to walk a spiritual path, that's the best intention we can have; and we're creating very good kamma with it. The intention is already a success, all by itself. The more often we take the trouble, the more help we will get in meditation from this good kamma.

We also immediately get a second result: the recognition of what's going on inside us. As soon as a disturbing thought comes forward, we observe that our mind is rather wild and untamed. This is an important realization, because previously we had no idea what sort of mind we have. As we label them, we notice the negativity of the thoughts and possibly also their egocentricity. All this is success, the kind of success denied to someone who doesn't meditate.

The next step brings a further result: as soon as we begin meditating, we turn to the object of meditation. This turning is the first factor in every single meditation. At the same time it's the polar opposite of sloth and torpor. We can't turn to the object of meditation until we have overcome both of these. This is the third of the five hindrances we all must face (desire for sensory satisfaction, ill will, sloth and torpor, restlessness and worry, skeptical doubt). The Buddha describes it as a prison. The laziness of the mind aims to prevent us from meditating today— after all, tomorrow is another day. It wants to stop us from getting up early, and it refuses to recognize the truth because it's too uncomfortable. These factors of torpor—mental laziness— must disappear for a time so that we can recognize the object of meditation and stay with it. It's a hindrance because it has the effect of imprisoning us until we are able to concentrate. Then we free up energy so that the mind can regenerate itself. This mental laziness is also a hindrance in everyday life, when every-

thing becomes too much for us, when we tire easily and let ourselves be distracted from what's really important. Laziness of the
mind leads to weariness of the body.

The more often we fight against this laziness during meditation, the easier it will also be in our daily life. Mental laziness
must be combated through self-discipline. Since everyone has to
face this third hindrance, there's no reason to blame ourselves for
it. But we should recognize what is really right and important in
life. And so every time we sit down to meditate or engage in
meditation while we walk, we can always record at least one
result: we have acted against the laziness of the mind.

And so the fourth immediate result is present if we can stick
with the object of our meditation. This means that we have to
remain seated long enough to let some peace come into our heart,
and for the concentration to last a while. This result counteracts
the fifth hindrance, skeptical doubt, which is present in everyone
too. Everyone feels uncertainty about whether this is the right
way, whether we have to meditate, whether we will ever manage
to do it, and whether we should follow the words of the Buddha.
Was he really enlightened, and can someone still become enlightened nowadays? Might not the people who just want to amuse
themselves be right after all? This recurrent doubt is very damaging, because it holds us back from devotion. We reserve our opinion for ourselves and accept only bits and pieces of what we hear
or read, whatever confirms our opinion. Unfortunately, not much
can come of this mixture, because it doesn't add up. Every personal opinion is based on the illusion of ego: "I think—I believe—I am—I will . . ." This can never be the absolute truth,
not even the relative truth, because we're constantly changing our
opinion.

Skeptical doubt holds us back from devotion and causes us to
pick and choose the parts of a spiritual teaching that seem acceptable to us. But a teaching is a unified whole, and the teaching of
the Buddha is a complete organism; it's made up of individual
parts. But it can blossom only when all the parts are included. It's
like a jigsaw puzzle: if we only see a piece here and there, the
entire picture will never be visible. Only when all the parts have

been fitted together can we make out the picture. Our doubts and uncertainty make it impossible to see the whole, because uncertainty makes us drag in our own views. So we can't follow the path with our whole heart, because it takes trust to do that. Skeptical doubt is exactly the opposite of trust. But in the moment during meditation when we have once experienced calm, we know: This is right. This is what I've been looking for. And so the coarsest doubt falls away.

Now trust in our own spiritual capacities begins to emerge. This moment is also important insofar as it helps us to continue on the path without being held up by mental laziness. Through the first two steps of meditation we acquire such great advantages that we have to be grateful simply for being allowed to practice. The Buddha compared skeptical doubt to a person wandering in the wilderness without supplies: he runs around and around in circles and is finally slain by bandits. We run around in circles in our constant quest for happiness; we doubt this or that until the spiritual path has finally vanished into thin air.

In daily life too we are bothered by doubts and uncertainties. We don't know exactly what the most important thing is, and we feel overtaxed. If we find ourselves in a situation we don't like, we often see no way out. These doubts can be traced back to the fact that we still haven't found any clear direction in ourselves. But if we do find it, at long last, and are ready to grow spiritually, to purify our emotions, and to continue on the path of meditation, then we also know what to do and what really matters whenever we're in a doubtful situation.

Skeptical doubt, which we feel not only with respect to the direction of our life, but toward ourselves as well, is based on a lack of love. If we can devote ourselves in love, then doubt will be eliminated, because doubt is charged with hatred. When we sit down to meditate, we should love being there, just to be helpful to ourselves. We can be glad that we are allowed to sit and meditate, and thus have a possibility of growth. We should also love our breath, for without it we couldn't live. With this attitude toward breathing and sitting, our meditation should run more simply. Doubt and love can't exist side by side. We always doubt what we don't understand and don't love. When we love, there are no doubts. When we realize that our breath and meditation deserve love, because both are so immensely helpful, we make life easier for ourselves.

The hindrances consist of human qualities that everyone has within himself or herself. It's important to recognize how they make life harder, because they bring chaos into our internal household, from which our life takes its cues. We are certainly interested in keeping our external household in order. We definitely make our bed and wash the dishes, so that a certain peace and quiet will prevail in the house. But it's much more important to maintain order in our inner household to truly promote the growth that we care about.

Our own inner household is constantly in difficulties, because the five hindrances turn it topsy-turvy. When we recognize them and acknowledge that they're hostile to us and will never do us any good, we'll bar the door to them. After all, we invite into our house, the place where we live, not our enemies but only our friends. We may begin with the hindrances that we combat immediately and automatically through meditation: with sloth, torpor, and skeptical doubt.

By now we have succeeded in taking four steps: the initial turn to the object of meditation, continuously addressing it, patience, and contentment. Then we cast aside laziness and doubt, so that the qualities can arise that make it possible for us to come to rest.

Now comes the first step of meditation itself. The method is only the key without which we can't open the inner gate. The object of meditation has to be firmly fixed in the mind in order to find the keyhole. After we insert the key, turn it and open the door, we enter a house with eight rooms. The feeling we experience when we enter the first room is *pīti*, which is roughly equivalent to rapture. One might conclude that this room is rapturous. But the point here is rather the capacity to hold the object of meditation concentrated in the mind long enough so that we come into contact with inner purity, because we have succeeded in not thinking. Thinking veils the purity that exists in all of us. Initially it will take some time before we get into touch with this purity. But later, when we are more practiced in meditating, it can happen right away. This awareness of our own mental purity produces a feeling of rapture, and sometimes ecstasy, because it's an altogether wonderful physical feeling.

But during meditation we have no interest in the body, only in the feeling, in perception. This is so wonderful that it leads to an intense interest in meditation. That interest is so strong that we'd like to go on meditating, with no desire ever to get up again. Hence *piti* is sometimes translated by "interest." This sensation is strong enough to completely eclipse any physical discomfort that may have been present before. It's the beginning of the meditative absorption, or jhāna, that opens up to us levels of consciousness totally different from those we knew before. The first four levels of these jhānas, the first of which is pīti, are called fine-material absorptions, because they have a certain similarity to conditions that we know from daily life. They are, however, much stronger, and in addition they're independent of the world. They depend only on our concentration.

We have all had pleasant physical sensations. But every one of them was caused by external circumstances. Here we have become independent. The first moment of this independence is the first moment of freedom. We aren't yet perfectly free from external circumstances, but the first step has been taken. So long as we are dependent on worldly things and other people, we are their slaves and we let ourselves be shaped by them. We always have to take care of something "out there." We have to be richer, handsomer, younger, or smarter than others. But none of that is important. What we really need is concentration, to be able to raise our mind above the world. The longer we practice, the easier it will be to have patience without expectations, to devote ourselves trustingly, without thinking it over. Here's a motto I like to use: Don't think—do.

Pīti is aimed at especially unpleasant hindrances: ill-will, anger, hatred, rejection. These are sensations that result in only one thing: making life harder. The more we have enjoyed the pleasant feeling of pīti during meditation, the lower our level of ill will. (The Buddha compared ill-will to gallbladder disease. It's no accident that we say, "That galls me!") There is only one medicine to cure this: love.

If we succeed in finding the entrance to our inner castle in meditation, that will bring about an automatic purification, which greatly eases the work on our anger and ill will. The comparison that the Buddha offers is that someone who acts out of anger is picking up hot coals with his bare hands and throwing them at someone else. The absurdity of such an action is obvious.

The entrance into *jhānas* is the first step that liberates us from this disturbing, painful thinking and shows us an interior world that we had always hoped for. We may have sensed that it exists. We may have believed that if we could find someone whom we could love and who loved us in return, we would pull it off. However, to our alarm we discovered that this didn't bring us inner peace and harmony. We get there only by making drastic changes in our heart.

Without spiritual help it's extremely hard to transform the phenomenon of hatred in daily life into love and compassion. But if we know that at any time we can get to delight through meditation, then not only does purification automatically set in during meditation, we also see a reflection of it in our daily life. If we have never awakened this feeling, we don't know that it's present in us. But just knowing about it gives us more security. We have within ourselves everything that we long for. The only things that we find outside are the means to keep our body alive, such as food, drink, and the necessary money. What we really want, the things we really long for, are hidden within us.

Our thoughts, reactions, hopes, plans, and opinions make it hard for us to find our way to concentration. So long as we think and plan and are busy with ideas, our ego sees itself confirmed. Even if this confirmation consists in dukkha, that's still a confirmation, which is why so many people cling to their problems. In meditation we have to let go of our thinking and our problems, in order to get to our delight. So we have to temporarily give up our self-centeredness, which is why concentration is difficult. But once we realize that the ego isn't so important, and that as soon as the meditation is over we can look after it again, then it may be easier for us to drop it for a while. One helpful decision here would be: "I really want to concentrate now—woolgathering isn't important." With this decision, we can direct the mind exclusively to the object of meditation; we can enter upon the inward path.

Inner rapture is immensely valuable because it contains so many positive results. We now understand that what the world has to offer isn't remotely comparable to what we already have within us. This makes renunciation considerably less difficult. We no longer have to run after every pleasure, constantly meeting new people, seeing and hearing remarkable sights and sounds. We have something far more valuable and satisfying. That doesn't mean that we can't enjoy a beautiful sunset anymore—quite the contrary. We can do that much more easily and purely, because we are thankful that this too has been given to us, along with the happiness that we already have experienced in ourselves.

The joy that we have in earthly things goes through a purification and now has a different quality. Every human mind that devotes itself to meditation, that has patience and continues to practice it without expectation, can find inner rapture, because that's the natural path taken by the human mind.

From a practical standpoint, the moment when breathing has become so fine that one can barely sense it is the moment when we can make the transition to inner perception. The question whether these perceptions are the right ones isn't even asked, because they are so delightful that they overshadow everything else. In addition, the Buddha recommends that we combat rejection, anger, and hatred in everyday life as well by continuously developing loving-kindness in ourselves and replacing the unhealthy with the healthy. Loving-kindness meditation is comparable to mental training that serves the cause of thinking and feeling rightly. Meditative delight is an enormous help in shaping our daily practice more simply. It might sound to some people as if it's hard to get there, but it's only a matter of time and patience. Every human being wants to take this path, whether he or she knows it or not. Everyone would like to bring the mind to rest and experience his or her interior life as something beautiful.

Please put the attention on the breath for just a few moments.

Think of all the nice things you have ever done in your life, such as helping another person, being concerned about another's welfare, being loving and kind to another one, giving a present. Anything that you can think of that you think was a good thought or deed. Remember it now. And then feel warm and loving toward yourself, recognizing all the goodness in yourself.

Think of the people who are close to you. Think of all the good deeds that they have ever done—those that you know and those that you surmise. Appreciate them and love them because of that goodness that you can feel in them.

Think of the people you know. Let them arise before your mind's eye. And think of all their good deeds that you know about or that you surmise in them. Feel your heart going out to them. Appreciating . . . loving . . . respecting the goodness in them.

Think of those people who are part of your life but toward whom you feel quite indifferent. You meet them here and there. You don't have any real connection to them. Think of all the good things they have done, possibly for you. Appreciate and love them and respect them. Make your heart reach out to them.

Now think of anyone whom you don't like or who is bothering you in any way, and then think of all the good things that person has ever thought, said, or done—whether you were actually present or not. Appreciate and respect that person for his or her goodness. Let your heart go out to him or her, feeling the oneness that unites all of us.

Think of people in your hometown: those you know and those you don't know. Remember all the good things you know about them, surmise the others, and appreciate them; let your heart reach out and connect with their hearts.

Now think of people everywhere: in the towns . . . in the cities . . . in the villages . . . in the countryside. All of them are looking for happiness. All of them have goodness in their hearts. Connect with that goodness, connect with their hearts. Let your appreciation, your warmth and respect for all these beings flow out of your heart and help to lift the consciousness that is present in humanity.

Now put your attention back onto yourself. Feel the ease that comes when consciousness goes to goodness and lovingness. Feel how the mind feels lighter, pleased, carefree, and the heart feels loving. Connect with the goodness in yourself. See it clearly. Anchor that recognition within your heart, so you can retain it. Never lose sight of it. And feel the appreciation and warmth welling up within you, connected to that goodness.

May all living beings feel love and devotion.

7. THE NINTH FRUIT
The First and Second Jhānas

THE FOUNDATIONS OF MEDITATION are moral behavior, guarding the sense doors, mindfulness, and contentment. The Buddha sometimes described these four as the roots and trunk of a tree. If the roots and trunk aren't healthy and strong, the branches, leaves, and fruits won't be satisfying either. Thus these four form the groundwork on which we can build.

The immediate results of meditation, even if our concentration is still weak, are the creation of good kamma through intention, insight into our own thoughts, countering the laziness of the mind, and setting aside doubts and uncertainties. These are the rather common advantages. The first higher result that the Buddha called a very visible fruit of renunciation is the first meditative absorption—the first jhāna.

Renunciation plays a great role in absorption. The Buddha explains absorption with the words "Secluded from sensual desires, secluded from unwholesome states of mind." In order to get to the first jhāna, we have to renounce these things—at least during the time of meditation. The more we have already gotten used to this letting go in everyday life as well, the easier it will be for us during meditation.

The Buddha used the image of a bath attendant who soaks soap powder in water and makes a ball of soap. Just as this ball of soap is drenched with water, we are drenched with rapture from head to toe. At the end of absorption we must observe how impermanent even this wonderful sensation is. At first it will flare up only briefly, as if to show us that there's more to all this than watching our breath.

When this gratifying event happens for the first time, the mind, unfortunately, reacts at once, either with astonishment or joyful excitement; and this destroys the concentration. Probably the mind, after losing its concentration and this rapturous perception, will anxiously hope to be able to reexperience it. And that is going right back to clinging and wanting to have. Hence, even if the feeling has lasted only a second, we have to realize that this pleasant feeling too is transitory, and so we have to work against impulsive reactions. If we absolutely insist on having the feeling, if we go on searching for where it may have come from, then we won't experience it again. It came about through concentration. If this concentration lasted long enough, a certain purification was achieved, because for a time no negative thoughts or sensual desires were present. There was neither craving nor hatred, and so it was possible to make contact with the purity of our own heart. But as soon as wishing enters it again, this condition becomes impossible, because desire is present once more. Thus at the end of this first jhāna we must always look at its unstable, changeable nature.

We have to acknowledge how this lovely feeling slowly dissipates. The next reflection should be to recapitulate the path that we have taken in order to reach the first jhāna. Here almost everyone will discover something that was different than during earlier meditations. This is usually so minimal that it's almost unnoticeable. Perhaps we ate differently or tried a different method of meditating. We have to recapitulate in order to clearly recognize the path. When we know, we can take it again. So long as it's still a matter of luck, we aren't talking about *sammā-samādhi*, right concentration. Thus there are two things needed at the end of the meditation: to recall impermanence and to recapitulate the way.

Of course, the transitory nature of pleasant feelings isn't something we wish for, as it is with the unpleasant ones. Only when we can look at transitoriness and react to it with calm have we found spiritual equilibrium. We have also acquired understanding: since we could clearly observe arising, we also can concentrate on ceasing.

One important point of this first jhāna is the fact that it can come about only because we have temporarily abandoned any ego confirmation. Unfortunately, it frequently happens that we do reach the first jhāna and its wonderful sensations, but that our thoughts nonetheless intrude. This is nothing but ego, which keeps wanting to have its say. The more we learn to abandon this ego, the deeper our meditations get, and the easier the next steps will be. The insights that these next steps afford us don't have to be laboriously worked up. They come about automatically when the jhānas succeed. This is the easy, cheering path to enlightenment. Sometimes this way is described as difficult, but that's incorrect. In all his guidelines the Buddha describes the jhānas as steps on the way, as means to an end. If we stick to the directives of the great master, we find here the possibility of attaining not only serenity and peace, but also an incomparable inner joy.

This inner joy is called *sukkha* in Pali and is directed against the fourth hindrance, restlessness and worry. This fourth hindrance is significant, because we often don't recognize it. Restlessness is a hindrance that isn't completely overcome until we reach full enlightenment. Through the jhānas, however, restlessness is diminished insofar as we come to rest and many of our wishes fall away. We find more peace in the heart. Restlessness exists when we are unfulfilled; thus we are looking for something to satisfy us.

In worldly life this quest may take the form of traveling, changing our occupation or partner or residence—or any kind of external change that continuously awakens the hope of fulfillment in us. We can readily recognize this sort of restlessness as we drive around looking in vain for a parking place. Everybody is in transit. Thousands of people are in transit, day and night, because of this restless lack of fulfillment. If we sense joy during meditation, then restlessness decreases, because we know that we can turn inward again at any time, toward this happiness that fulfills us. During meditation cares and restlessness are laid aside because we can't simultaneously concentrate and be worried. Through the repeated act of letting go, the hindrances get smaller.

It's like weeds: when we do nothing in the garden, the weeds smother all the beautiful plants. Weeds rob the other plants of nourishment, of rain and sun, and if we can't eradicate them because their roots are too deep and powerful, we can at least cut them back so that they get smaller and weaker. And that's exactly what happens through the meditative absorptions. We don't uproot the hindrances, but we make them smaller. When our understanding has finally gotten clear enough, we can uproot them. Most men and women have to admit that they still get angry even after regularly meditating for many years. Even if we understand the process intellectually, if we wish to emotionally comprehend equanimity, we need new feelings, otherwise we remain stuck in the old ones. The new feelings of meditative absorption automatically purify us. In the process we find an interior life we didn't know before, and everyone senses that inside himself or herself there's something beyond the duality of wanting to have and wanting to let go.

Hence we practice and learn to concentrate on our breath, because through it we discover an interior world that is not only pleasant and desirable but also enables us to stop taking the external world so seriously. On no account do we become indifferent—quite the contrary. But we're on the way to serenity, and that means to finding peace. With the second jhāna we let pleasant bodily feelings retreat into the background, in order to direct our attention to the emotion of joy. Therefore we turn away from the coarser sensations toward the more refined ones. The Buddha compares the feeling in the second jhāna to a lake into which neither rain falls nor streams flow but that nevertheless is filled by the upwelling of cool, clear water from a deep spring. Just as the cool, clear water totally permeates the whole lake, the joy of the second jhāna totally fills one's being.

The fourth hindrance, restlessness and worry, is compared by the Buddha to being a slave, for when we succumb to our cares, we cannot master our life. We have neither control nor peace; we are trapped in the world of our thoughts. As an antidote for everyday use, Buddha recommended turning more and more to the dhamma. When we have enough knowledge about the teaching, we will recognize possibilities that are not self-centered and that hence give us peace.

Furthermore the Buddha mentions yet another effective remedy for all the hindrances: noble friends and noble conversation. Conversation is a part of our mental nourishment. Supplying physical nourishment is relatively uncomplicated, but we have to plan very carefully for the feeding of our minds.

Noble friends are people who aren't just good friends, but also worthy men and women who strengthen what's good in us. If we surround ourselves with hate-filled, greedy people, that will definitely rub off on us. We're all susceptible, and so the Buddha repeatedly advises us to get close to the right people—the sort of friends who are trustworthy and loyal, who stick with us through good and bad times, even when they don't agree with us. A noble friend bears love and kindness in his or her heart and is always at our side, even when we don't ask. We'll gain this sort of good friend only if we ourselves are such a friend. We can learn to be a noble friend ourselves. The Buddha praises noble friends and noble conversations as "the whole of the spiritual life." In other words, we should associate with those who support and accompany us on our spiritual journey, who are already a few steps ahead of us on the path. But that isn't absolutely necessary, for in any case good friends are those who strengthen us in goodness.

Yet another factor of the jhānas is the one-pointedness that counteracts the desires for sensual gratification, which is our greatest hindrance. The hatred that we bear within us is, of course, most unpleasant, but it's easily recognized; and if only we stop trying to justify it, we can gradually get rid of it. It's a totally different story with sensual gratification, which all of us are worried about as a matter of course. That seems altogether appropriate, because what are all those beautiful and pleasant things for, and why shouldn't we treat ourselves to them, if we can afford it? Why not make ourselves as comfortable as possible? The mistake in this way of thinking is that it puts no limit on "pleasant." We keep having to set out anew in this direction, because nothing remains the way it is—including the pleasant things. That way we never come up with enough time or energy to follow the spiritual path consistently, to make it worthwhile.

The king tells the Buddha that with the fruits of professional work one can clearly see the gain. But where's the fruit in the case of meditation? This is a perfectly reasonable question. One doesn't become aware of this gain until one practices actively. The Buddha compares our sensual desires to the situation of a debtor who has to pay monthly installments with interest. If he's lucky, he'll manage to pay off all his debts before he dies, assuming he doesn't incur any new debts. But we never get finished with the desires of the flesh—not even on our deathbed. Even there we still want to get comfortable, although that's probably not possible. In order to handle sensual desires we have to deliberately put an end to them. But we can't do that until we've noticed that they bring us nothing.

Naturally this doesn't mean that we should stop eating, sleeping and looking at beautiful things. That would be irrational, and the Buddha's teaching is realistic. We will just refuse to spend our time, energy, and money making ourselves as comfortable as possible. Hedonism is so widespread in our culture that we don't even notice it, because it's viewed as the norm. Only an impartial observer can recognize this, and so we ought to ask ourselves whether we shouldn't let go of many less important things that only claim time and energy that could be put to better use. The Buddha recommended analyzing the things that we want to have, taking them apart and looking at the individual pieces. If we did, we'd clearly see their impermanence; we'd refrain from many of our efforts and give up many of our wishes. That would appreciably lower the level of dukkha, because the fewer wishes we have, the less dukkha.

Of course, this wanting-to-be-comfortable is also aimed at our emotions. We would much prefer to meet with the sort of the people who give us constant confirmation, but no one succeeds in doing that. We have to realize that the unpleasant things are impermanent too, that new emotions keep coming up, and that we can have little influence on the nature of other men and women. We can only work on our desires. Since desire for pleasant things, if it isn't met, immediately unleashes hatred, it's enormously important to realize what we are doing, and to counteract our desires by analyzing them. We will notice that everything is without permanent substance, without meaning. We will stop getting angry at so many things and stop racing after every wish.

The one-pointedness of meditation helps us to concentrate, and it excludes all sensual desires. The more often we meditate, the more we weaken sensual desires. We crush the weeds, even if we can't yet rip them up. The jhānas too are worldly mental states. Mental conditions above this world will be achieved through insights; the jhānas make it possible to broaden the mind so that it has an easy time reaching insights.

The second jhāna concentrates on the feeling of happiness, and initial and sustained attention to the breath is no longer necessary. Rapturous physical feelings remain in the background, joy and one-pointedness in the foreground. The second jhāna gives us self-confidence, since our happiness no longer depends on anything external. We aren't waiting anymore for someone to make us happy. We don't need to buy anything else, or travel anywhere—we have discovered happiness in ourselves. We have become independent, and our self-confidence is strengthened thereby. We no longer lose our heads in unpleasant situations; we face things with peace and serenity. Self-confidence is often taken for arrogance by outsiders, because the world around us is like a mirror. People without self-confidence can't recognize it, because the mirror can only reflect what we show it. Independence brings a feeling of freedom with it.

The Buddha explained that the meditative absorptions in their highest form are states that give us a foretaste of *nibbāna* (Skt. *nirvāna*), as we sense what it feels like to be without an "I." The "I" can never become happy. It always has some wish or other. But in the jhānas, when the "I" is thrust aside, we can just simply be happy. This releases a stronger urge to go on practicing, because anyone who has mastered the jhānas and meditates using them will be rewarded with insights and can hardly stop practicing. Understanding what we experience is necessary, of course; and the knowledge that nothing lasts will make the further absorptions and insights that must be achieved easier for us.

The Buddha called the advantages of the first jhāna a visible fruit and those of the second a still higher visible fruit. This gain is increased with every level of absorption. We become aware of this through our inner vision. A person who experiences the jhānas will readily recognize another person who does too, without having to talk about it. The practicing of these absorptions expresses itself emotionally in our inner life. It also remains present in our everyday routine and sheds its luster on it.

8. THE NINTH FRUIT
The Third and Fourth Jhānas

WE NOW TURN AGAIN to the meditative absorptions, the jhānas, even if we can't manage deep concentration yet. The Buddha always said that growth, which ultimately leads to perfect freedom, is a gradual process. We have already had an intensive discussion of the first two jhānas. In the third, joy and pleasant bodily sensations are now ignored, and all our attention is aimed at the contentment we feel. In the third jhāna we are happy without wishing for anything. This is a sense of letting go, of sinking more deeply into ourselves. That is in fact what happens, because the first two jhānas are played out, so to speak, "farther up," where "up" means something not quite as subtle. We are talking about an inner sensation that every individual can create for him- or herself.

The jhānas can be reached with patience, perseverance, and confidence, and ultimately they become something we take for granted. The world looks the way it does because the human race thinks it knows what peace is and how to achieve it. But that's as grandiose an error as the notion that each one of us is an "I." We succumb to the false expectation that others will somehow or other manage to conjure up peace—an absurd expectation, of course. Everyone can only make peace in himself or herself by letting go of all discord. In the third jhāna we experience a foretaste of what it means to have peace. Our wants and wishes have to be let go of, because even the least of them brings us nothing but discord. Meanwhile, we're usually not satisfied with small, inconspicuous wishes—who wants to be small and inconspicuous? That's the most important component of the third jhāna: we can't experience it unless we really want to be nothing and have nothing.

It's quite clear that each jhāna provides deep insights if we turn our mind to it. If we don't, at least we are still going through a process of purification, if not of insight. In the third jhāna the mind rests and plunges into the depths. The other factors of absorption are weakened, wishes have disappeared, and there is peace. Our wish to survive does seem fully justified; but it prevents inner peace, because we refuse to accept the fact that survival simply isn't possible. Every other wish also creates an unpeaceful state. In any case we all want to be something definite—not just anybody. If for whatever reason this wish isn't fulfilled, our hearts become conflicted. The only peace that we can find lies in ourselves. And until we have sensed it in us, we won't be able to find it in the world.

Naturally it's not enough just to seek—and find—peace. Without understanding we won't manage to maintain peace in the daily jumble of demands. If we care at all about this, and if we want to know a more peaceful world, then we have to give up wishing. Just talking about it doesn't help. If we want to give the world a little more peace, we have to possess it ourselves in order to pass it on. If we feel peace in ourselves, then the people who come in contact with us will sense that instantly. Very few men and women on this planet have found peace in themselves, and so we don't live in a peaceful world. During the Christmas season there's talk about it everywhere, but by January it's all been forgotten. The words make sense, but the talk and the action are very sharply different.

Without the meditative absorptions it's hardly possible to find the way to peace. They give us a method, but then we also need the opportunity to practice this path. Getting such an opportunity is the best thing that can happen to us. The next time we sit down to meditate, we should realize that we've gotten this opportunity only because we have acquired a great deal of good kamma. That's an authentic reason for joy, which in turn is an important aid in our ability to concentrate. The utterly normal joy over something beautiful in our life helps us to concentrate. Once we have gotten this, it's followed by pleasant physical sensations and in the next step by the meditative joy that spreads an inner sweetness around itself. With the third step we get to peace and contentment. Although the mind is prepared for it, it's still an impressive, deep-reaching experience. The crucial difference between this and other methods of altering our state of consciousness is the process of purification, which has already taken place. When a state of consciousness is altered by chemical or other external means, the mind isn't prepared for it and can't achieve deep insights. As a result, the state may not be maintained or repeated at will, and the inner purification has no support.

If we have arrived at inner peace through the third jhāna, then we can carry over something of this into everyday life. Our mind is a jewel that bears the seed of enlightenment within it. The Buddha explained the third jhāna with the following metaphor: in a lotus pond many different lotus flowers bloom, with many different colors. There are flowers that grow up out of the water, and there are others that remain underwater. The ones underwater are totally saturated by the water—their blossoms, their leaves, and their roots are completely soaked. It's exactly the same with the inner peace and contentment of the third jhāna. We are saturated with it in such a way that we can sense it from top to toe.

In order to reach the fourth meditative absorption, all joys and sorrows are let go. At the moment of moving from the third to the fourth jhāna, this only means letting go of peace, but we must also have already developed equanimity. We must recognize that the purpose and end of meditation is not to find inner peace, although we may have always viewed that as the goal. But if we manage to hold on to inner peace long enough, it will become increasingly clear that this can't be all there is. With the first three jhānas there was always an observer in place: the ego. But the mind has become more subtle and knows what's what. It sees clearly that peace, joy, and above all the observer have to be abandoned too. Entering the fourth jhāna is comparable to sliding into a deep well, where one sinks deeper and deeper. The person whom we know has now willed to give himself or herself up and to sink into this deep well.

The fourth jhāna has various stages. In the beginning our concentration is still such that we can hear sounds—granted, not as disturbing, yet nonetheless there. But if we reach the bottom of the well, then we no longer hear anything. There is such a profound silence that we can barely even recognize the observer, although he or she is still there as much as ever. Only the silence remains, as described by the term "equanimity." The word for equanimity in Pali is *upekkhā*, which refers to one of the seven factors of enlightenment. For us equanimity means a quality that excludes excitement.

But this explanation is inadequate for the fourth jhāna. Now that we are "submerged," our "I" is no longer recognizable, because it has "gone under." Two things are especially important for the fourth jhāna: one is the fact that this absolute rest regenerates the mind so dramatically that it can be called the mental fountain of youth. The clarity of the mind becomes a shining star. The mind has finally found an opportunity to rest completely. This new power of the mind makes it clear that the problems people have are caused by thinking and reacting. Besides, we can experience a level of consciousness without dukkha, which is possible only without ego or ego consciousness.

Of course, immediately after meditation this ego consciousness returns to its usual place, but the belief that it has to remain that way forever vanishes. Finally we have a foretaste of how things can be without ego-consciousness—and it is splendid.

On the subject of the fourth jhāna, the Buddha has given us the following comparison. A person is wrapped up from head to foot in a white cloth, with not a single spot uncovered. That's how it is with this silence. We feel ourselves fully swathed in it.

The first four jhānas are summarized in the following parable: a thirsty man is wandering through the desert and can't find water anywhere. Thus we seek fulfillment through external influences or through faith in some external power, but our thirst isn't satisfied. Now if we see in the distance the glimmer of water, we are joyfully excited and head toward it. This is pīti, the first jhāna. Filled with joy that the desert isn't waterless after all, we stand on the shore of the lake. This is sukkha, the second jhāna, for now we know where our thirst may be quenched. After we have drunk our fill, a state of wishlessness arises, because we're perfectly content. This is the third jhāna. We've found what we were looking for, and are full of peace. Now we lie down under the nearest tree and rest. This is the fourth jhāna. This resting fills us with new strength and energy. This is a clear and simple representation of the path that we can follow. We all thirst for the water of life.

The more we let go of the ego, the easier it gets. All those who practice with perseverance and don't let themselves be disturbed by the things that the mind wants to force on them can take this path. And unconsciously every mind would like to do just that. Since we all have a portion of infinite consciousness in us, there's absolutely no reason why one person should be able to do it and another not. Everybody can do it. We all have the same human mind. So it's a question of purification, of kamma, and self-discipline.

The Buddha divided people into four types:

There are people who, when they meditate, experience a great deal of physical, mental, and emotional dukkha, and make only slow progress.

Then there are those who experience dukkha of all sorts and make rapid progress.

In addition, there are those who experience a lot of sukkha and hence have a great deal of joy while practicing. They are doing well, they are content with their state of meditation, and they also feel no pain. But it takes a very long time before they achieve anything.

Finally, there are those who experience much joy and in addition make very rapid progress.

It's impossible to predict which group anyone belongs to, but there are certainly mixed groups too, people who experience dukkha at one time and sukkha at another. Therefore we have to comfort ourselves with the knowledge that with patience and perseverance it's possible for anyone to follow the path.

There is a nice story about a man from Rājagaha, who sought out the Buddha and told him that he had already been listening to his discourses for ten years and in the process had gotten to know many monks and nuns. Some had changed quite positively during the ten years; they had become loving, wise men and women, while others had changed for the worse. These individuals were filled with hatred and malice and had no wisdom at all. But all of them had heard the same discourses—so how could they have reacted so differently? The Buddha answered the man with a counterquestion: "Where is your home?" The man said: "I am from Rājagaha, but now I live in Benares." Then the Buddha wanted to know: "Do you ever visit Rājagaha, your hometown?" "Oh yes," the man declared. "I go back all the time; I have family and business there." The Buddha then inquired: "Do you know the way there?" "I know the way so well," the man replied, "that I could find it in the dark." The Buddha continued: "If someone came to ask you how to get from Benares to Rājagaha, could you explain it to him?" Full of conviction, the man said: "I know the way so precisely that I could describe it to him in the minutest detail." The Buddha then said: "I am sure you could. But if you had described the way quite exactly, and the man who asked you stayed in Benares and didn't set off on the road to Rājagaha, would that be your fault?" "Not at all," the man indignantly answered, "I was only the signpost." Indeed," said the Buddha, "that's what I am too."

The directions are clear, but we all have to take the path ourselves. The only thing that changes us is what we ourselves have experienced. This experience, once recognized, can never be lost.

9. THE NINTH FRUIT
Fifth, Sixth, Seventh, and Eighth Jhānas

THE FIRST FOUR ABSORPTIONS are called in Pali *rūpa-jhānas*. *Rūpa* means body, and *jhāna* is absorption. These fine-material absorptions fill us with joy, rest, and peace. The fine-material absorptions are called that, not because they are physical sensations, but because in living in the material world, we have all experienced states of rapture, joy, contentment, and equanimity. But these experiences during the jhānas are much more sublime, much more refined. Thus they are referred to as "refined experiences from the ordinary world" or "fine-material absorptions." The boundary lines we normally experience so sharply become blurred and the heaviness disappears.

These first four jhānas are followed by the four *arūpa-jhānas*, with the *a* translated as "not." Thus these are the immaterial (formless) absorptions that are purely spiritual and have nothing to do with any conscious states we have known before. They are located completely outside the sphere of our usual knowing. They are described as a continuation of the fourth absorption, but they sometimes appear quite spontaneously after the third. With every step that we take, the mind is prepared for the next one and thereby becomes ever more subtle.

The first jhāna gives the mind a perfectly natural power that leads without strain or effort to the further jhānas. But the Buddha doesn't say that we should wait until something spontaneously happens, only that we should divert the mind to the next stage. That is, we should deliberately start opening ourselves to the next step.

The fifth jhāna leads our consciousness into a feeling of infinite space. With the first jhāna we are dealing with bodily feelings, and this is somewhat the case even with the fifth. A feeling of infinite expansion of the body can emerge till there are no more limits, and the infinity of space becomes the only thing consciousness can make out. The Buddha gives the following explanation for this: If we see a house, we can imagine that a village is there. We can perhaps see a whole village and a single tree, and then all the other trees. Thus we can soon imagine the entire village, the woods, indeed the entire country and the whole continent, and still more and more until everything disappears, and only the entire space of the universe remains in consciousness.

Some people will get to a point where the body can stretch no further and infinite space is not yet recognized. Here we are talking about an intermediate stage; and we can imagine the sky without a horizon, so as to experience infinite space. Other people experience infinite space without any intermediate stage. In this infinity there is nothing—no person and no "I." And this is the knowledge that, by means of this experience, lends us a whole new vision of ourselves.

The first three immaterial absorptions are the great insight-absorptions that open the way to clarity and liberation. Here our own experience is decisive; nothing else can lead to liberation. After the experience of space, worldly things don't affect us so much because we have experienced another truth. Perhaps arrows will still be shot at us, but they won't hit us so hard because we have become smaller targets.

After the sphere or realm of infinite space comes the sphere of infinite consciousness. This is only logical, since infinite space can't be known except with an infinite consciousness. When mindfulness is turned toward infinite space, consciousness is completely impersonal. There is no one to whom it belongs, no one who is fenced off. The only thing present is a consciousness of infinite expansion. There follows a recognition of the infinite consciousness, which is aware of the infinite space and which is fully impersonal.

Normally our consciousness is shriveled up. If it's full of hatred, it's totally shriveled up. By contrast, if it's full of love and kindness, it extends as far as our love reaches. If this love is only for a single person whom we wish to cling to, consciousness is only slightly extended. The more our love embraces, the further consciousness can expand. Thus loving-kindness is a necessary factor to give meditation scope and breadth. And the more we free ourselves from ego, the further consciousness can expand and reach toward infinity, where self-centeredness has no place. But this doesn't mean that enlightenment has been achieved, that the ego has been given up for good. We have simply experienced how it's possible to put aside this troublesome ego for a time. So long as we still believe in our ego, we also believe in a personal consciousness, in our own ideas, plans, wishes, and hopes. We believe that all this belongs to us and that it must make sense because we thought it up ourselves. Only when a person has taken some steps in meditation will he or she realize that thoughts and all the things they elicit are nothing but trouble. The more we abandon this little point in the universe—the "I"—the broader and more flexible our consciousness will be.

Let's recall that the jhānas are comparable to a house with eight rooms. While staying in one room of the house, we may decide to visit another one, but we can also stay put. The decision to go into another room means inclining and aiming the mind in that direction. This decision opens up our consciousness to something new and prevents the rejection of what can't be grasped by the senses.

The mind alters its direction so that it can take the next step and turn from the infinity of space to the infinity of consciousness. As soon as the sixth jhāna has repeatedly been experienced we come to realize that there are no differences between people, because we no longer perceive any separation. That makes it much easier to apply loving-kindness, and we have once again experienced the process of purification.

Insight into absolute truth is still closed to us. We can't recognize it because of our clinging and aversion. In order to be able to meditate we have to free up this foreground so as to arrive at the background. The background isn't the subconscious, because we know precisely what happens in meditation. We know what it's about, but we must take each step ourselves. Although the Buddha offered metaphors to help describe the first four jhānas, that comes to an end here. Now the body no longer plays a role. We don't become conscious of it again until we have ended the meditation. In the infinity of space and infinity of consciousness, an especially striking feature is the temporary experience of *anattā*—non-self—the final result of the spiritual path. To be sure, it takes constant practice for us to approach this knowledge not just intellectually but emotionally.

Since this experience is far preferable to our everyday life, it's clear how much more simply we can live without the "I." *Anattā* doesn't just mean "non-self," although that's the literal translation. It also means insubstantiality, which we find in everything when we observe absolute truth. We practice and live on two different levels, because it's impossible to do otherwise. We live in relative truth, which is also quite real. There everyone has his or her name, is either male or female, has a specific age, a specific profession and an appearance that distinguishes him or her from others. All this exists in relative truth, and here everyone tries to find his or her happiness, but it never really works. On this relative level are flowers, statues, houses, trees, grass, water, sky, stars—simply everything. On this level we try to achieve purification, to develop mindfulness, to practice loving-kindness, and to concentrate. Sometimes this all succeeds; at other times it doesn't. But everything that we learn has only one purpose: to lead us to absolute truth. Individual things and separations don't exist there. The only thing that is there is something scientists have known about for decades: not a single solid building block— only particles of energy that coalesce and then dissipate.

The scientists who recognize this fact would all be enlightened if they had included themselves in their findings. Unfortunately they are only observers. For those who have really experienced what has been proved, written, and taught, the picture of the world changes. They can't be threatened by anything anymore, because what can happen to a particle of energy? It joins another particle of energy and then goes off again. That is how the world looks on the absolute level, and these two stages of meditation— the sphere of infinite space and the sphere of infinite consciousness—help us to experience this. It's impossible not to sense a change after this experience. Of course, even people who practice the jhānas still have to deal with the relative world, because our body can't transcend the material level. Only the mind can do that. But the meaning of everyday things is evaluated differently, and the awareness that everything passes away takes us to a level on which clinging diminishes.

The meditative absorptions lead to the realization that the "I" isn't a separate reality, that it has no core, that there is only the whole of creation. The meaning of the jhānas is to build a foundation for becoming aware of the emptiness of all things. This can hardly be understood in an intellectual sense. But if we experience an infinite space and an infinite consciousness where there can be no separation and no individual existence anymore, the idea of absolute emptiness begins to dawn. Many religious and spiritual disciplines don't deal with absolute emptiness, because they view it as a fatalistic nothingness. But this is a false reading. Heart and mind do not become perfectly empty, but they are penetrated by the absolute truth that there are no individual persons, only unity. This experience has been described in detail by the medieval Christian mystics. There are many different paths leading to the same realization.

The seventh jhāna is called the "sphere of no-thingness." A simple comparison may help us to understand what it means. When we enter a room, we see many things in it. There are pieces of furniture, cushions, flowers, people, curtains, and so forth. After we leave that room, imagine that someone comes in and removes all these objects from the room. Then when we return to the room, this once-familiar space is absolutely empty. The room is still there, but it's empty. This gives us an experience of the void. Through our practice we have gotten to a point where we no longer need things so much and can let go of them. We no longer need to cling to anything. Everything can quietly become empty.

In meditative stillness we experience now and again a movement of contraction and expansion. This is the real movement of the universe, which is constantly in the process of contracting and expanding. Our body does the same thing, and when we have become very mindful, we can also experience this in meditation—in a true and profound meditation. This is also the mystery of people who can pass through walls or levitate. They have translated into reality the fact that there is nothing but particles of energy that come together and then disperse. We are all of us nothing but that. It's comparable to the waves of the sea: here too there are small, medium, and large ones. They all dissolve—even the biggest.

It's impossible to experience these levels of consciousness in the jhānas and not change. We know that our milieu has a formative effect on us. Thus if we experience the jhānas as heightened and expanded states of consciousness, and we frequently repeat them, we'll also get a changed consciousness in our everyday world. Jhānas three, five, six, and seven are insight-jhānas, while the eighth jhāna leads neither to consciousness nor to the unconscious. It is called the "sphere of neither perception nor nonperception." It's similar to the fourth jhāna, which gives us new mental energy. This happens to a still greater extent in the eighth jhāna, which excludes the observer so much that the experience can be discerned only after the fact. The eighth jhāna excludes perception so thoroughly that we cannot even recognize the infinite depths of rest present in it.

Now, there is also the trance state. But this is easily distinguishable from the jhānas: people who awaken from trances are dead tired, while those who come out of a deep absorption are wide-awake and full of energy. In a trance state the mind hasn't remained one-pointed; it has entered a thick fog. This can't happen to someone who is meditating and who has systematically entered the jhānas; but people who meditate without any guidance could possibly be "foggy-minded," because they don't know exactly what's going on.

Those who have taken the path of all the jhānas, from the first to the eighth, have to know every step precisely. Then they can learn to go forward and backward, even to leap from one jhāna to another. To be a master of the jhānas, consciousness and concentration have to be so strong that one can enter any absorption at any time. One determines how long it will last and afterward can describe exactly what the experience consisted in. The Buddha said about the jhānas: "It is impossible to calculate the breadth of influence of a person who practices the jhānas."

Even if such a person sits in a cave and pays no attention to worldly matters, he or she has a powerful influence on what takes place in the world. The jhānas prepare the mind to become supple and ready to internalize the different stages of insight. In this way it can experience absolute truth.

QUESTIONS AND ANSWERS

Q: If there's nothing but particles of energy, how can you distinguish between good and evil?

A: The particles of energy are found on the level of absolute truth, good and evil on the level of relative truth. On the level of relative truth, where we live, it's generally our conscience that tells us what is good or evil.

Q: Where does our conscience come from?

A: Have you ever taken a good look at your conscience? See where it comes from. Where does the wish come from to experience something other than the everyday world? Just examine how this arises. These things are part of human beings when they allow themselves to listen and to look at themselves, and consider the inner life more important than the outer life.

Q: When does the ego die?

A: It was never born and it can't die. It's the illusion that dies. The jhānas are the means to the end, not an end in themselves. We've thought up the ego, which is forever making problems for us. Our job is to emotionally let go of this way of thinking.

Q: What does *Buddha* mean?

A: Buddha is not a name. It means "The Awakened One."

Every Buddha rediscovers for himself or herself the core of the teachings, the Four Noble Truths along with the Eightfold Path. An enlightened person who applies the teaching of the Buddha is called an Arahat. The Buddha was an Arahat too, an Enlightened One, but also a Buddha.

10. THE TENTH FRUIT
Insight, Cause, and Effect

THE BUDDHA DESCRIBES the jhānas first because after them the mind can be successfully directed toward understanding. But even when we haven't yet succeeded with the jhānas, a fairly successful concentration is enough to create the possibility of reaching insight. One metaphor imagines a sharp-eyed person looking at a jewel whose facets are perfectly polished and whose purity is untroubled. With his unusually sharp eyes he recognizes a thick red thread running through this otherwise perfectly pure gem. That's how the Buddha explains our capacity to recognize even the tiniest imperfection, when the mind has come to rest and so has been unusually sharpened.

Hence we should always use the concentration acquired through meditation in order to attain understanding. But not everyone can take the same path. On this point there's a story about Ajahn Chah. This venerable teacher taught in northern Thailand, and many Westerners came to him. One of these critical listeners once put the following question to him: "How is it that the pieces of advice you give sound quite different? One time you advise a specific meditation and another time an altogether different one. What am I supposed to think?" The teacher responded: "If you meet a motorist who always drives too far to the left, you'll no doubt warn him to steer more to the right, so that he doesn't drive into a ditch. But if someone else drives too far to the right, you'll surely tell him to steer more to the left to avoid an accident."

So one person should drive more to the right, the other more to the left. It's quite simply a matter of what's happening to a person at the moment. Thus one approach isn't good for everyone.

But through concentration, and above all through the jhānas, the mind is sharpened and comes to see connections that it wouldn't normally recognize and that it would otherwise reject. That's why in his discourses the Buddha always explains the jhānas first and the insights afterward. The term *insight* has a special quality in the Buddha's explanations. It means "looking into oneself or into something," and not just "understanding something." It means anicca, dukkha, and anattā—impermanence, unsatisfactoriness or discontent (pain in general), and insubstantiality. These three characteristics of existence are summarized under the term "understanding," with each of these qualities including the other two. Once you have comprehended one of these, you'll be familiar with all three.

Thus everyone is free to choose for closer inspection whichever of the three distinguishing characteristics he or she wishes. Someone with a trustful, and hence loving, heart won't be very anxious about impermanence, and will explore it first. An analytical person will first explore insubstantiality; and someone who finds concentration easy—amazingly there are such people—will first observe dukkha, or pain. One of the most important methods of insight is recognizing the five aggregates of clinging, or khandas, which consist of (1) the body, (2) sensory consciousness, (3) feeling, (4) perception, and (5) mental formations and reactions (thoughts). The Buddha explained that we are made up of these five parts—there are no others. We don't simply have to believe this or reject it: we should put it to the test. Meanwhile we have to know that belief is based on craving and rejection or hatred. If we believe in something sight unseen, craving is at work, in that we want to make things as simple as possible for ourselves. We believe and follow the opinions of people with the same views. That way we spare ourselves the trouble of analysis.

It's easier to spot the link between rejection and hatred. When we reject something, we don't want to know about it. We don't need it, and we condemn it in advance without wanting to know what we're condemning. The Buddha recommends choosing the middle way—scrutiny. A person who believes easily has it easier because he or she also loves easily. On the other hand, a person who rejects easily has a harder time of it, because he or she also hates easily. Nevertheless the rejecting person has one advantage: he will notice in his heart an unpleasant feeling that prompts him to look more closely to discover the truth. The credulous person feels quite comfortable and won't sense this urge to the truth. In examining the five aggregates, we will find that, contrary to our experience elsewhere, the expression "aggregate" doesn't refer to anything solid; it's nothing but a collection of gathering and dispersing movements. If it weren't that way, we would have to remain forever just as we were born, without change or development. Everything is constantly in motion—which we admittedly know, but which doesn't bother us.

Yet if we just concentrate on that, we'll sense this motion in ourselves. We're subject to the same error as the one we make about our mental qualities. Sensory perceptions likewise seem to be complete and unique. We see, we hear, we taste and smell. In reality this is a matter of wave movements, as with radio and TV. For example, when our eye glances at a visual object, actual seeing begins. We never get the idea that this isn't really an action of the eye but a continuous up-and-down motion of tiny particles. But that has been scientifically proved and we could readily inform ourselves about it, should we so wish. It's the same with hearing. There is no possibility of "solid" hearing.

The Buddha recommended that we strengthen our mindfulness and develop equanimity, so that all things can appear in a different light. The light in which we see ourselves, and the quality that we know of ourselves, is solidity. Our body seems to be a solid mass that can see, smell, hear, taste, and touch. The sense perceptions then give us feelings—pleasant and unpleasant—that we have to react to. If we want to gain understanding, these connections must be clearly recognized so we can set aside all the pain that our existence contains. We have to realize what we are made of. We can do that only when we approach this understanding. Then we can grasp the fact that there's nothing in the universe but movement. Having learned that, we can keep our reactions in balance, in a mental equilibrium where exuberance and depression no longer have the upper hand. In everyday matters we act as we did before, but the reactions have changed. We can tell other people who practice from this quality. This mental equilibrium should never be confused with indifference. Because they are similar, indifference is called "the near enemy" of equanimity.

In exploring the five khandas, the mental formations will probably cause us the greatest difficulties. Are they solid or are they constantly in motion? Are they joyful or painful? Where is the "ego" actually located? Scrutiny of the ego, which is supposedly contained in mental formations, is especially interesting to people with an analytical bent. Since our birth we have already had millions of mental formations, and this "I" must have been changing from second to second. So it can't possibly be solid. Then what does this changeable "I" look like? Where is it to be found? We have to grasp these important questions meditatively because the intellect finds countless arguments for and against.

Each one of these five aggregates is marked by the same qualities: arising and ceasing. The impermanence of mental formations will strike us when we investigate them. We know that there was something important there, and we go to a lot of trouble to recall what it was. We regret not having written it down—it was so important! This makes it quite clear how these mental formations are subject to constant disintegration. A mind that has already found its way, through meditation and concentration, to a bit of rest can accept this transitoriness and constant fading because they become clearly recognizable in meditation. Everything trickles away.

Examination of the five aggregates helps us to let go. Letting go is the main quality of spiritual life. The more we cling, the more material we are. Attachment is the material quality of the wish to have and hold. By contrast, letting go is a spiritual quality that we can practice on both a large and a small scale. Some day, perhaps, we may even be able to let go what we call "I." We'll be forced to do so anyway, like it or not. On our deathbed we'll have to give up the "I." If at that late date we still don't want to, we'll have a painful struggle with death.

We should fight out this struggle now while we're in full possession of our mental and physical energies, by learning the different meditative stages of letting go. It's been said that if we have already practiced it, the moment of death will provide us with the final learning experience, with what could be a special triumph. Thus it's important to explore the five khandas. Even if some questions remain unanswered for the moment, it's helpful to ask them, because that way we can let go of some of this absolutist thinking, to which we're all prone, and which continuously tricks us into believing our wishes, by claiming, "I just want to have things a little more pleasant; and if I tackle the situation a bit more cleverly, and go about it somewhat more skillfully, things will work out." That's how our own views go— and those of the whole world. But it's all just an illusion. Nothing will happen unless we have experienced it internally, recognized it, and worked it out ourselves. That working out is the most fascinating prospect that life affords, and it leads to great gains, as the Buddha informed the king who wanted to know what the advantages of spiritual life were.

Of course, physical work is necessary to keep our body alive, but getting mental clarity is incomparably more valuable. That way we enter a domain where we look upon all the daily responsibilities merely as sidelines, just as we don't consider it our main task in life to wash our face and brush our teeth in the morning.

The teaching of the Buddha is sometimes called the teaching of cause and effect, or the teaching of analysis, but most usually the Middle Way. This Middle Way is always a balancing act that no one can take over for us. Cause and effect have several meanings. The first reference the Buddha makes to the five khandas is the fact that we can determine why they came about, what their causes and effects are. The cause of the body's existence was our urgent wish to be a human being on earth—the desire for being. We can see this in all plants and trees. In California there is a Monterey pine that grows all by itself on a rock in a lake. How far did this tree have to send down roots to make its own life possible? We call this the life force or vital energy. The Buddha called it the "desire for becoming." We want to be, and so we come here. We come to conception as rebirth-consciousness. So we mustn't reproach our parents, because we sought them out for ourselves. That's how the Buddha explains it.

We have to understand that we are dominated by a consciousness that wants to remain alive, that wants to return to life, and that therefore has asserted itself. This is the triggering mechanism of the body. Among the proximate causes of the body are the nourishment and care we have to provide to it. When we get very thin, we haven't eaten enough, and when we get too fat, we've overdone it. If something in our body isn't functioning properly, we feel pain. Thus everything is built on causes. The same thing holds true for the four aggregates of the mind.

When we take the body as cause, we have the five senses as effect. If the eye functions normally, it attaches itself to sense objects. If the eye were sick or if everything around us were gray on gray, then the eye wouldn't see. But if visual objects are present and the eye is healthy, seeing comes about as the effect of these causes. From seeing as a cause comes feeling as an effect. This isn't easy to recognize, but when we concentrate on what sort of feeling, for example, a beautiful flower produces, we can tell that it's a pleasant feeling. And so the body is founded on the desire for being. Feeling comes about through sensory contacts, which are followed by the effect of perception that recognizes and names. So this is the cause of reactions such as wondering whether the flower has a name—Is it for sale? It's probably very expensive, and we won't be able to afford it. Which brings us to the bank, because we have an account there. These trains of thought in turn trigger more feelings, so that we move in a continuous cycle of cause and effect. If we investigate this, we'll probably continue to feel the effects, but some day we'll be fed up with them, and so we'll direct the causes onto other tracks.

There is yet another cause-and-effect combination that must be looked into: *kamma*. The Buddha said that kamma is intention. Literally translated, *kamma* means action. But the Buddha clearly indicated that kamma isn't just action, it's intentional action.

In our usage we also call the results of action kamma, although that in itself isn't right, because we have used only one word for both cause and effect. It is essential to examine this law of nature. Under no circumstances should we fall into the error of thinking that kamma is simply what happened in an earlier life when we were Persian dancers, Egyptian pharaohs, or Roman soldiers. That's the past—and it's irrevocably gone.

Kamma as cause and effect can be examined only in the present life. What sort of consequences present events will have in a later life is likewise totally insignificant, because what exists is the present moment. The only life we can ever have, regardless of what's happening, is this one moment. The past is a memory, and the future is a hope and a dream. What we really experience is this moment—now—and it's already gone; the next one is already gone too. If we don't look out, they'll all pass us by, and we'll find ourselves wondering in the end: What did I actually do over all that time—those sixty, seventy, eighty years? The point is to live this one moment and to understand kamma as cause and effect now. Here too it's hard to recognize the connection because, as the Buddha said, kamma is linked together like a spider web, where we can make out neither beginning nor end. We can, however, open up to the knowledge that we don't feel good when we have a negative feeling and cling to it. So we have to drop it, since it's the cause of our uncomfortable feelings. Once we grasp that, it becomes clear that we can never again blame everyone else for what happens to us.

Everything that someone else does is his or her kamma; we can't change this in any way. We have our own kamma, and it depends entirely on our thinking and action. If someone heaps abuse on us, it's as if he were picking up burning coals to throw at us. It's entirely up to us whether to duck them or let them hit us. In any case, the person concerned has inflicted pain on himself or herself. We had no influence on it. But to spare ourselves bad kamma, we should always react with sympathy for everyone who harms himself. No one can prevent another person from taking on bad kamma. The only thing we can do is never lure anyone into acquiring bad kamma. Once that's quite clear to us, we begin to be careful.

We must view kamma on two levels. A person who has set

aside the illusion of ego can't create any more kamma. But anyone who still carries the ego illusion around is creating kamma, because he believes that he himself is thinking, speaking, and acting. How far old kamma has consequences for us we don't know, but obviously it has some. Otherwise we wouldn't be citizens of a specific country, be practicing this specific profession, and so forth. But it's much more important to know that we have free choice whether we wish to do good or evil. This free choice is crucial, because it opens up the possibility of taking the spiritual path. Kamma is an impersonal quality—neither punishment nor reward, but simply cause and effect.

If we get aggressive and attack someone, we have to reckon with that person's defending him- or herself. If, on the other hand, we react lovingly, we can assume with some certainty that we will be given similar treatment. Thus we are not rewarded or punished; we are the authors of the effects that we ourselves initiate. It's not simple to understand the impersonality of kamma, because every one of us knows people with quite evil characters who are nevertheless doing well, and others who are very lovable and helpful, yet constantly in difficulty. Naturally we view this as injustice, and we even reach the conclusion that the universe is ruled by chance.

But that's not right, as we know from the fact that night follows day, that the earth spins evenly and unstoppably on its axis, that everything that is born must die. Only our understanding is chaotic. Kamma is a perfectly clear succession of interconnected causes and effects.

The Buddha explained kamma with the following image: If you put a teaspoon of salt into a cup of water, it becomes undrinkable. But if you pour that teaspoon of salt into the Ganges, it makes no perceptible change in the river. So if you put a teaspoon of bad kamma into a cup of good kamma, there's a dramatic change. But if you pour that teaspoon into a whole river of good kamma, there'll be no perceptible difference. That's the source of what appears to us as injustice, but it is only a consistent course of events.

We have the possibility of continuously exploring the quality of our thoughts, words, and deeds. Selflessness brings good kamma. Unfortunately, when we do something good our motivation isn't always pure and selfless. We have to look into this so that we don't lie to ourselves. In any case it's better for all sides when we do something good, even if the intention behind it isn't completely selfless. As soon as we recognize that our heart feels lighter when we do good, the easier our life will be and the clearer our thinking.

We live in the cycle of cause and effect, and when we plan the first step to leave this eternal cycle behind, we have to stop reacting to our feelings. That sounds simple, but it certainly isn't. We have to keep on trying, and above all we have to remember that when we succeed in not reacting to feelings, we have called a halt to hatred and craving.

These two things make our life infinitely hard, above all because they're so often disguised that we don't recognize them at all. They are our enemies, even if greed often looks quite handsome. Hatred, of course, always remains ugly, but it has the mighty weapon of justification. Once we have recognized the maliciousness of these two companions, we will keep on ejecting them from our heart, so they can no longer poison it. The more insight we gain into the ego illusion, the easier it will be to get rid of hatred and craving, for both of these are effects of the ego illusion. They arise from the ego illusion, and the smaller this cause becomes, the smaller too its effects.

11. THE FOUR HIGHEST EMOTIONS
Loving-kindness, Compassion, Sympathetic Joy, and Equanimity

MOST OF OUR PROBLEMS are concerned with interpersonal relations, as was the case with King Ajātasattu. Hence we direct our view once more to the four divine abodes, which are called in Pali *brahma-vihāras*; they are loving-kindness, compassion, sympathetic joy, and equanimity.

If we had only these four emotions at our disposal, we would have paradise on earth. Unfortunately that's not how it is, and so we rarely experience any paradisiacal feelings. Most of the time we torment ourselves with difficulties in the family, in our circle of friends, and on the job. Our mind constantly tells us about all the things that don't suit it; and it usually fingers the guilty party, the person who's bothering us, who doesn't want things the way we want them. But let's remember: whenever somebody else says or does something, it's a matter of his or her kamma alone. Only a negative reaction on our side creates our own kamma. So long as we haven't fully and completely accepted this fact, we will keep on creating negative kamma. It's simply not possible for the whole world—much less all human beings—to be oriented to our satisfaction.

As long as we react negatively, it's only logical that the negative results won't be long in coming. We generally can't comprehend this at all or only with difficulty. Why is that? Purely and simply because of defective practice. The longer we practice, the easier it gets. Only when we notice how much we harm ourselves with negative reactions will the idea flash through our head that it's really foolish to hurt ourselves. And with this awareness we can begin to observe our reactions more mindfully and, step by step, to change them.

Of course, we can always stick with the notion that the only ones responsible are other people, and we can pity ourselves. But this sort of behavior leads more and more deeply into dukkha. When we sympathize with ourselves, we are literally "suffering-with" ourselves. And we're a long way from realizing that such suffering arises from ourselves alone.

As a matter of fact there's nothing more logical and reasonable than to acknowledge that the outside has nothing whatsoever to do with what's going on inside us. But we keep believing that the world has shot an arrow at us and scored a hit. Of course, that's because we want to defend our "me." Once again, unfortunately, we haven't understood things properly. There is a protection for the "me," but we can't find it in other people who are supposed to love us, recognize us, understand or admire us and, besides, confirm how valuable we are. Sadly, this doesn't work, as we have all no doubt already discovered. As soon as we have acknowledged that everything depends upon our loving and recognizing others, we begin to really practice. If someone loves us back, that's wonderful; but it doesn't make the least difference in our own capacity to love.

This is what we absolutely have to understand: who is doing the loving—myself or the other? If I myself love, then I have a certain purity of heart. But if the love is dependent on this or that person or situation, then I'm passing judgment and dividing people into those I think lovable and those I don't. And if someone who I used to think was worthy of my love displays even one single reaction I don't like, I'm finished with that person and cross him or her off my list. My thoughts in this case will run something like this: "How wrong I was about so-and-so. I thought he was wonderful, and now look what he did." We act like a judge who is always on the bench passing judgment. Most of the people we sentence become "lifers." We don't want the condemned to come near us again, ever. It's obvious that such behavior can never bring rest and peace, and yet it's utterly typical of all of us.

We're all looking for an ideal world, but it can exist only in our own heart, and for this we have to develop our heart's capacity so that we learn to love independently. This means that we increasingly purify our heart, free it from negativity, and fill it with more and more love. The more love a heart contains, the more love it can pour out. The one and only thing that holds us back is our thinking, judging mind. Thus, if we educate our heart to love, we'll know what it's like to perceive love. Then we no longer need someone who loves us, because we have enough love in our hearts. And so we've become independent of other people's emotions, which gives us security. Dependency leads to uncertainty, since we can never know for sure how things will turn out. Anything may happen to the other person. He or she might love us or stop loving us. He or she might die or remain alive, be friendly or in a bad mood. All that's uncertain, and throws us into uncertainty. Hence we want everything to stay the way we consider acceptable; and it's this very wish that causes dukkha—suffering. As long as we expect someone else to do something that appeals to us, we'll suffer, because we want to have something and may not get it. Interpersonal relations are difficult not just with partners or family members, but in any situation where people come together. This is because of our inner judge. So long as we sense the "me" in us, it's impossible for our views to coincide all the time with those of other men and women: everyone reacts to sense impressions in his or her way. For example, in somebody's front yard there are stones that one passerby thinks suit the place marvelously: everything is so tastefully arranged. Meanwhile another person is horrified and wonders what kind of people dump rocks in front of their house like that. So, absurd as it sounds, a real dispute might erupt over these stones.

Thus it's impossible for all of us to be of the same opinion, because the "me" that everyone lavishes care and attention on colors and discolors everything. There are the memories, the circumstances we grew up in, professional biases, and the people in our milieu—all of this influences our views. If we wish to search out the ones who agree with us and recognize only them, our capacity for love remains very slight.

So the only thing that matters is to incline one's own heart to love, because the person who loves is by nature lovable too. Yet if we love only because we want to be endearing, we succumb to the error of expecting results for our efforts. If an action is worth doing, then it doesn't lose this value, whether we get results or not. We don't love as a favor to another or to get something. We love for the sake of love, and so we succeed in filling our hearts with love. And the fuller it gets, the less room there is for negatives.

The Buddha recommended looking upon all people as one's own children. Loving all men and women as if one were their mother is a high ideal. But every little step toward this goal helps us to purify our hearts. The Buddha also explained that it was quite possible that we already were mothers to all the many men and women. If we keep this fact before our eyes, it'll be much easier to get along with people, even those who don't strike us as lovable.

If we observe ourselves very carefully—and that's the point of mindfulness—we will find that we ourselves are not one hundred percent lovable. We will also observe that we find more people unlovable than otherwise. That too can bring no happiness. So we should try to turn this around, and find more and more people lovable. We have to act like every mother: she loves her children even though they sometimes behave very badly. We can make this sort of approach our goal and recognize it as our way of practice. The Buddha called this kind of love *mettā*, which is not identical to what we call love. "Craving" in Pali is *lobha*, which sounds rather like the English word for love; and because the entire world revolves around wanting-to-have, we also interpret love this way. But that's not love, because love is the will to give. Wanting to have is absurd, when we think of love and yet degrade it to this level. Although a loving heart without wishes and limits opens up the world in its purity and beauty, we have made little or no use of this inherent capacity.

The far enemy of love is obviously hatred. But the near enemy of love is devotion and clinging. Clinging sounds nice, as if it were something good. But if we take a closer look at this expression, we see that we're not standing on our own two feet and giving love; we're holding on to someone. It often happens that the person we cling to doesn't find it especially pleasant and would be glad to get rid of this clinger, because he or she can be a burden. And then comes the great surprise that the love affair isn't working—but we clung so devotedly! Clinging is thus called the near enemy, because it looks like real love. The big difference between the two is the possessiveness that marks clinging.

Such possessiveness proves, time and time again, to be the end of love. True, pure love, so famed in song and story, means that we can pass it on and give it away from the heart without evaluation. Here we have to be on the lookout to recognize the negativity within us. We're always searching for its causes outside ourselves, but they're not there. They always lie in our gut and darken our heart. So the point is: Recognize, don't blame, change! We must keep replacing the negative with the positive. When no one is there to whom we can give love, that doesn't in the least mean that no love exists. The love that fills one's own heart is the foundation of self-confidence and security, which helps us not to be afraid of anyone. This fear can be traced back to our not being sure of our own reactions.

If we meet someone who has no good feelings to bring our way, then we already fear a corresponding reaction on our side, and so we prefer to avoid such situations in advance. But if the heart is full of love, then nothing will happen to us, because we know that our reaction will be completely loving. Anxiety becomes unnecessary when we've realized that everyone is the creator of his or her own kamma. This feeling of love, which is aimed not at only one person, but forms a basis for our whole interior life, is an important aid in meditation, because only through it is real devotion possible.

The second of the four divine abodes—the highest emotions—is compassion, whose far enemy is cruelty and whose near enemy is pity. Pity can't give others any help. If someone pours out her heart to us and we pity her, then two people are suffering instead of one. If by contrast we give her our compassion, we help her through her trouble. It's very important to develop compassion for oneself, because it's the precondition for being able to do so for others. If someone doesn't meet us lovingly, it will be easier for us to give this person compassion instead of love. It's easier because now we know that this person who comes to meet us unlovingly is angry or enraged, is most definitely unhappy. If she were happy, she wouldn't be angry or enraged. Knowing about the other's unhappiness makes it easier for us to summon up compassion, especially when we've already done so with respect to our own unhappiness.

Unfortunately we often deal with our own dukkha in the wrong way. Instead of acknowledging it and meeting ourselves with compassion, we try to escape our trouble as quickly as possible by developing self-pity or getting distracted or making someone else responsible for it.

Here compassion is the only possibility for meeting our difficulties. We experience exactly what the Buddha teaches: in this world dukkha exists. That's the first Noble Truth. Then we can try to acknowledge what we really want to have or get rid of, and thus make dukkha our teacher. There is no better one, and the more we listen to it and find a way into what it's trying to make us understand, the easier the spiritual path will prove. This path aims to change us so emphatically that in the end we may not even recognize ourselves.

Dukkha is a part of our existence, and only when we accept that and stop running away from it, when we've learned that dukkha belongs to life, can we let go—and then the suffering stops. With this knowledge it's much easier to develop compassion for others, for dukkha strikes everyone, without exception. Even the so-called badness of others can't bother us, because it only arises out of ignorance and dukkha. All the evil in this world is based on these two things.

The third of the four highest emotions is sympathetic joy, whose far enemy is envy, consisting of greed and hatred. The near enemy is hypocrisy, pretending to oneself and others, which we believe is sometimes necessary. We think: these are just little white lies that can readily be forgiven.

Sympathetic joy is rightly understood when we see that there's no difference between people, that we're all a part of whatever is momentarily existing in the world. So if one of these parts experiences joy, then its joy has come into the world and we all have reason to share in it. The universal will replace the individual when we have experienced and tasted it in meditation. Our problems won't let up so long as we try to support and secure the "me." Only when we begin to put the universal over the individual and to see our purification as more important than the wish to have and get, will we find peace in our hearts.

The Buddha called the fourth and last of these emotions the greatest jewel of all: equanimity. It's the seventh factor of enlightenment, and its far enemy is excitement. The near enemy is indifference, which is based on intentional unconcern. By nature we take an interest in everything. We would like to see, hear, taste, and experience everything. But since we have often been disappointed by our incapacity to love, we build an armor of indifference around us, to protect us from further disappointment.

But that only protects us from loving and opening ourselves to the world of love and compassion. What clearly distinguishes equanimity from indifference is love, for in equanimity love is brought to a higher development, while in indifference love is not felt at all or cannot be shown. Equanimity means that we already have enough insight so that nothing seems worth getting worked up over anymore.

How did we reach this understanding? We've learned that everything—above all ourselves—comes into being and then passes away. When we get too excited, instead of recognizing the fullness of life, we don't yet have a loving heart. Only a loving heart can realize the fullness of existence. The understanding we get through meditation clearly shows us that the end of this life is constantly before us. Teresa of Ávila said: "Not so much thinking—more loving!" Where does thinking get us? To be sure, it landed us on the moon. But if we have developed love in our hearts, we can accept men and women with all their problems and peculiarities. Then we'll have built up a world where happiness, harmony, and peace are in control. This world can't be thought up, it must be felt. Only meditation can present us with this ideal world, in which it is absolutely necessary to give up thinking. This heals us and gives us the capacity to turn more to our heart.

Since equanimity is a factor of enlightenment, it is based on understanding, above all on the realization that everything that takes place also passes away again. So what do I lose? The worst that can happen is the loss of my life. But I'll lose that in any event—so what's all the excitement about? In general, the people who cause problems for us don't exactly want to kill us. They just want to confirm their ego. But that's not our business; it's wholly and entirely theirs. So long as we meditate and win new insights, it will always be simpler to recognize that all desire for self-affirmation, all aggression, all claims for power, all wanting to have and be are intertwined with conflict. So we have to keep trying to let go of willing and wishing, in order to return to equanimity. You can't meditate at all without equanimity. If we're excited or absolutely want to get or get rid of something, we can't come to rest. Equanimity makes both everyday life and meditation easier.

That doesn't mean that conscience should simply be set aside. We need only understand that this judge in our own heart creates nothing but conflict. If we really want to have peace, then we have to strive to develop love and compassion in our heart. Everyone can achieve this, because ultimately the heart is there to love, as the mind is there to think. If we renounce thinking in meditation, then we sense a feeling of purity. We develop purity on the spiritual path. If only one person develops it in himself or herself, the whole world will be the better for it. And the more people purify their hearts, the greater the gain for everyone. We can do this work every day from morning to night, because we are constantly confronted with ourselves—with all our reactions and with the mulishness that keeps us busy, because it has such a solid hold on our inner life. The more observant we are, the easier we'll find it to let go, until the stubbornness has disappeared, and we've become peaceful and happy.

This work compensates us with great profit and with a security that can be found nowhere else. At bottom we all know about the factors that make up the spiritual life, but acting in accordance with them is very hard. Loving-kindness, compassion, sympathetic joy, and equanimity are the four highest emotions, the only ones worth having. They bring us to a level on which life gains breadth, greatness, and beauty and on which we stop trying to make it run the way we want it to—on which we even learn to love something that we may not have wanted at all.

The Buddha spoke about a love that knows no distinctions. It's simply the quality of the heart. If we have it, we'll find a completely new path in life.

Questions and Answers

Q: I have problems with the phrase "motherly love."
A: How so?

Q: Children sometimes behave impossibly—and so do I, from time to time, because I just don't know any better. But so long as in our society mothers are supposed to have nothing but pure love to give out, we mothers play along and act as if we were always absolutely lovable. But the children notice that that's just pretense.
A: That's not quite true. Of course, even mothers sometimes behave very strangely. But that has nothing to do with love. It makes no difference what sort of mood or situation a mother may find herself in: the love for her children remains and doesn't disappear simply because at the moment she's especially tense or nervous. On the other hand, there's no room for loving unknown persons, because when you compare the feelings for your own children with what you feel for strangers, you quickly learn the difference.

Q: Isn't the wish for one's own children to be better than others often what makes people push them to the foreground?
A: There are all sorts of possible reasons why one's own children are loved more than other people. The reasons per se

are not so important. Once again we're talking about the attitude, "This is mine!"

Q: But then this is, after all, a status symbol. It's not love when I look at it this way: this is my child, and so I love him or her. In this connection you also have to look at how people show off with children, as if to say: Don't I have charming kids! They're much better at school than the others. They get much higher grades. All that doesn't have much to do with love.

A: No, it has nothing at all to do with love. You have to examine your own feelings toward the children, as they are today, and then your feelings toward other people. At that point the differences will become quite clear. Behind these differences lies the inner critic—the inner judge. Once we've cleared this up, we can begin to take the feeling that by nature every mother normally has for her children and apply it to others as well. That's the only thing at issue. Whether you were a good or bad mother is irrelevant. What matters is the difference between your feelings toward your own children and toward strangers. For those who don't have any children of their own and who may not be on the best of terms with their own mother, this idea won't be very helpful. But it can show the kind of distinctions that are made. We turn our heart, so to speak, into a dark closet, instead of filling it completely with love.

Q: For me there's yet another problem, but perhaps it's rooted in my own bad attitude. I've already tried to expand this love for my own family to others. For me it was always an elevating feeling, but I've found that my wife reacts with jealousy. I now wonder whose problem this is. Maybe I haven't shown myself to be sufficiently loving?

A: Right on both accounts. It is her problem, but perhaps you were in fact not loving, because you didn't explain what it was actually about.

Q: I really didn't do that.

A: It would probably be a great service in expanding your capacity to love if you would explain carefully that it flows to all people in the same way. Then it'll be understandable, and the problem will disappear, since she can see for herself.

Q: But what if you were to explain that to a person who's not on a spiritual path? Then it would be hard to explain the difference between loving and wanting to have.

A: If one of the two partners is not on the spiritual path, that looks to me like a problem. Talking about it won't help a great deal; probably the best way is to set an example by the way you live and to expand the capacity for love.

Q: In the meantime I also believe that occasionally it's de facto necessary to separate because the development of the individuals has led off in such different directions that their commonalities are lost.

A: That's right. If one were already close to enlightenment oneself, one could handle any situation. But since the great part of the path still lies ahead, there will be moments when it just can't continue as it has been. At this point it's important not to spread blame around, but to admit as lovingly as possible that one hasn't yet advanced so far on one's path as to be able to handle the situation. Your own anger or hatred would only worsen the situation. Unfortunately one can't always come up with enough love, compassion, and understanding to defuse the situation, and the hope of converting the other person is slight. That does happen in some cases, but as a rule the estrangement is more likely to be intensified through an attempt at conversion. It's really quite difficult when one partner embarks on the spiritual path alone.

Q: I wanted to say one more thing on the subject of motherly love: I think that everyone knows the feeling of longing for the unconditional love of a mother. Simply to turn this feeling around would be a helpful device.

A: That's a very good idea, which I can only endorse. But I should have mentioned fatherly love too, and I apologize if anyone felt neglected. Still, it's definitely very helpful if we ourselves translate into reality the longing for unconditional love that we all bear within us. As a small child probably almost everyone has enjoyed this unconditional motherly love, because otherwise small children wouldn't survive. And it's an eternal wish to go back to it. Instead, we should develop it in ourselves.

12. THE TENTH FRUIT
Fear, Danger, Urgency

By NOW IT HAS PROBABLY BECOME CLEAR that everyone wants serenity for his or her mind, and many people have already become angry because they haven't gotten it, because apparently others—or they themselves—were at fault. This is a false attitude. Serenity and insight, *samatha* and *vipassanā*, are the two directions of meditation, to which all methods are oriented. This is a path of practice and exercise. It has nothing to do with any sort of perfection, only with training. There are hours, days, sometimes even a whole year, when no serenity occurs during our practicing, but we get a whole mass of insights, so that we get the crazy notion that we've become enlightened.

Then there are times in which the mind is inclined to rest, and the insights appear rather sparsely. In general they aren't even noticed. But we're surprised to find that we can meditate so beautifully and yet keep losing our temper with other people. Then the insights are simply not there. Both situations have to be handled with care, so that we don't on the one hand paint a marvelous self-image because we have so many insights, and on the other hand grow discontented with ourselves because meditation is going well and yet nothing happens. Both serenity and insight are necessary. In principle it doesn't matter which we acquire first. The one and only important thing is practicing.

Now, it can happen again and again that the mind just doesn't want to become calm. Then we have to immediately apply an insight method: observe the arising and passing away of the object of meditation, and the arising and passing away of the mind that observes the object of meditation. The more often we observe that, the more subtle the mind becomes. It's not the same thing as distraction. Distractions always cloud the mind. We have to realize how even the self-observing mind is in constant motion. Thus, if no serenity comes about and it feels as if, with all the mind's shuttling back and forth, there's been a short circuit, we must immediately turn to understanding. The mind must be given a task; we can't let it simply wander about. If we've clearly perceived arising and ceasing, then we'll also notice that everything trickles away. Every mind moment vanishes. The careful observation of this continuous disappearance can easily trigger anxiety. Such anxiety comes from the ego: it doesn't want to admit that nothing solid exists, that everything comes and goes, and that our complete disintegration has been preprogrammed.

We don't believe that this process of decay has already started. After all, we're sitting here, beautifully solid, many of us even young and attractive. In reality everything continuously disintegrates, regardless of whether we're young or old. And that's exactly what we don't want to admit, because it means that in our efforts to give existence security and solidity we're just chasing a delusion. But the whole world does that, and we can't believe that we're the only ones who see through the uselessness of this strain—whereupon our anxiety level shoots up. So it can happen that we turn away from meditation and insight. True, many don't give up completely, but they also don't make any progress. As soon as it becomes conscious, this anxiety should be discussed with one's teacher. Eventually this step must be examined with insight. There can be no disputing that the issue here is fear of one's own death, the death of the ego, of the "me," of non-being.

We may have often fooled ourselves into thinking that our own death is not so important, that we just don't want our dear ones to die. But when one actually experiences deterioration, and has to face it, then everything looks utterly different. In principle we don't want to believe that we're already caught up in the process of decline and decay. We have to visualize our death because at this moment, of course, we're still alive. We may structure even this visualization so that we talk ourselves into thinking it's perfectly all right to die. But when we acknowledge our deterioration, panic can set in, and we have to make our way through it. It takes courage and decisiveness to experience and accept one's own death. Giving oneself up means finding oneself. We can't really live until we have fulfilled this task. That may sound like a Zen paradox, but everyone who has the strength to do this knows exactly what it means. The person who comes out of this experience is different from the one who went into it, because he or she has found the truth.

Fear is something natural, and those who can overcome it have taken a big step in understanding. This is a sort of "dark night of the soul," and those who let themselves be intimidated by it will have to keep confronting it until they either break down or are ready to let go of the illusion of the solid ego. All our lives we face the same tasks. If we fail, we can be sure that we'll go through them again under still worse circumstances until we realize what's at stake. On the spiritual path there's only one thing to learn: letting go. This is the answer to all panic attacks and anxieties: letting go. Those who have accepted impermanence and decay have overcome much of the fear of death. Our whole existence is threatened by dangers. The greatest threat is that with our negative thinking we may create bad kamma. And the danger of not always behaving ethically looms very large. Offenses against any precept can be triggered by countless sorts of temptations. Not until we have experienced insubstantiality will these dangers be wiped out. We are also constantly exposed to the danger of ego annihilation, either through bodily death or through emotional reactions to an apparent lack of ego support. Once we have recognized this, we can closely examine our own dukkha. What does it mean? How do we deal with unfulfillment and discontent? Do we behave in such a way that the dangers lessen? Or perhaps we repress them, momentarily calm ourselves, and quickly create fresh distractions. Have we realized that the danger doesn't lie in wait for us outside, but in our untrained and unpurified mind? Only when we have gotten that far does serious practicing begin.

All men and women, of course, are exposed to those dangers, and if we look carefully at our circle of acquaintances, it's easy to recognize how hard a time people have coping with these dangers, how unhappy they make themselves and others, and how enormous the resulting physical and mental problems can be. We can make good use of this as a mirror image of ourselves, without judging or condemning. We are all in the same boat. If we understand this common destiny, we'll notice that we are under constant pressure because we always want something. We have expectations of life and ourselves that can't be met. They make it impossible to feel peace, harmony, and happiness, which we actually view as our innate right. Of course, this expectation is false.

We have arrived here, on this earth, with six roots, three wholesome and three unwholesome. The roots of unwholesomeness are greed, hatred, and delusion; the roots of wholesomeness are generosity, love, and wisdom. The right to happiness is no more than an illusion. Experiencing peace and harmony is nothing more than a pressure that we exert on ourselves. If we were just a little bit smarter, if we only had a better boss or a different partner, we'd do fine. But we'll get nowhere until we let go of the three roots of unwholesomeness. And they are extremely real, not superficial ideas or thoughts. There are really deep forms of rootedness that are the reason why we came to earth as humans. If we lacked the three roots of wholesomeness, we wouldn't have come as humans. And if the three roots of unwholesomeness were missing, we wouldn't be human either. Hence our task in life is clearly prescribed for us: reduce the roots of unwholesomeness and strengthen the roots of wholesomeness.

We have to focus all our urgency on the practicing of the spiritual path. If we wait for the right point in time, we'll have thousands of other things to tackle, and we'll probably never begin. The urgency of purification must be renewed and followed up every day. Recognizing which of the six roots we are dealing with at the moment is crucial because we have to cut down the weeds or cherish and care for the flowers. One of the six roots is always at work.

Everything is impermanent, and everything continuously changes into something else. Such is the pressure of decay and renewal. This pressure of renewal is constant dukkha and attests to the inadequacy of existence. This also explains why we're restless and depressed. In the depths of meditation we'll realize this. Then we can accept and internalize the pressure of disintegration. And thus we recognize and confirm the ways in which existence falls short. That means we have taken a great step forward, which will draw many others after us.

QUESTIONS AND ANSWERS

Q: What are the six roots called in Pali?

A: The three unwholesome ones are called *lobha* (greed), *dosa* (hatred), and *moha* (delusion); the three wholesome ones *dāna* (generosity), *mettā* (love), and *paññā* (wisdom). The word for "root" is *mūla*.

Q: When I look back, I've had the experience that the further I go on the spiritual path, the more I have to be on guard, because the slightest inconsistency immediately has negative consequences. Earlier negative thoughts had less impact on me. The more mindfulness, cleansing, and purity are practiced, the greater effects even minimally negative thoughts will have.

A: That's right. You have to become more careful. It's like climbing a ladder: If you're standing on the lowest rung when you fall, there's no harm done. If you fall from the third rung, you might sprain your ankle. But if you fall from the highest rung, you could break your neck. Still, we're talking about just one misstep, regardless of whether we fall from the lowest or the highest rung.

Q: Sometimes you wonder whether you should go on at all.

A: Absolutely, but those who have already climbed up part of the ladder or mountain enjoy much better air up there, so one really shouldn't give up.

Q: I've gone through moments when I've told myself: if kamma works out this way, then I don't want to go on. But at some point you have to go on anyway.

A: Yes, it comes back. Don't forget one thing: if you've

mastered the jhānas in such a way that they're always at your disposal, they work like an automatic purification. The more often you use them, the more they purify. You couldn't go on living without them, because they've become a part of your being. Then the question "Should I do it—or drop it?" has gone forever. There's just no other way.

Q: From level to level one acquires more confidence in one's own capacities as a climber, and one increasingly believes that the ladder will hold, no matter what. You can find joy in that.

A: Quite right, but there's always the danger of a misstep, which on the first rung has no importance whatsoever, so that you may not even notice it. On the top rung things look very different. In such a case you notice: I could break my neck with a fall like that. Those are difficulties on the path that you put up with, because of the advantages. Hence the danger of a misstep, of your own negative thinking, of your own false statement that makes others unhappy.

Q: Does the reaction to an unwholesome thought keep getting stronger?

A: Yes, when someone has been practicing for a long time and has already purified himself, a single unwholesome thought will make a strong impression, so that he may be plunged once again into the dark night of the soul and is stricken with doubt, wondering whether he's done the right thing at all. A single unwholesome thought! Whereas another person who stands below and hasn't begun to climb yet, entertains countless unwholesome thoughts and doesn't even notice it.

Q: Yesterday we learned how we should behave when people speak ill of us. How should we react when we're physically attacked? Should we stand still or run away?

A: That depends entirely on the situation; but in principle, in this sort of case, bad kamma is at work, and you should avoid it if you can.

Q: Is absolute truth the only thing that's excluded from evolution?

A: The term *evolution* was coined by Darwin, who had nothing to do with the Buddha, of course, owing to the great gap of time separating their lives. Absolute truth is excluded from change. That's true, but evolution doesn't make sense in this context.

Q: You've said that we should contemplate death and experience it in advance. Isn't everything transformation? If we accept that and go with the flow, then clinging shouldn't be possible.

A: Shouldn't be, but often that's not how it is.

Q: Then in that sense death doesn't exist. It's often represented as a terrifying specter; but actually one wouldn't need to talk about it at all, if in fact it doesn't exist. From this point of view, the opposite doesn't exist either. There is a death of thoughts, of emotions, and so forth. But actually there is neither beginning nor end—it's a continuous flowing and transforming.

A: Those who have taken in this continuous flowing can meet all men and women with love, because they've set aside all prejudices; they can also turn what they know into action. We can get our knowledge from all sorts of books and feed our intellect with it. But turning this knowledge into action is another story; that would mean living in accord with what we know. That's hard work, for which we need practice.

13. RELEASE FROM THE THREE CRAVINGS
Sensuality, Existence, Ignorance

UNDERSTANDING AND ENDURING:
THE EIGHTFOLD PATH

WHEN IN OUR PRACTICE we come to the point of urgency, we have arrived at the beginning of wisdom. The Buddha calls this "wise reflection." This is an attitude of mind that is neither meditative nor contemplative but arises from both. Still there are two possibilities: wise and unwise reflection. If we haven't yet practiced enough, we'll often choose unwise behavior, because we're imprisoned in our usual patterns, which tell us what would be good and pleasant for us. We invest a lot of energy in order to get something pleasant. Once we've finally gotten it, we're usually disappointed and begin at once to look for something new.

Wise reflection begins by considering where the root of our difficulties might lie. When we seriously address that question, we won't rest content with the superficial knowledge that everything can be traced back to the ego and only the ego. That would be too simple and no more than accepting what we've read or heard. We have to give our own wisdom a chance. Of course, we use the Buddha's guidelines, but some day we'll make them entirely our own, because we've weighed them and seen them for what they are.

The Buddha explained that we harbor three strong cravings, three subliminal states that drive our thinking and acting. These three cravings are called in Pali *āsavas*, which literally means something that flows out of us. These are instinctive desires for sensuality, existence, and ignorance. They are the reason why our ego illusion causes so much disaster. We recognize this in a subtle way in all the people we meet. If one of these drives is strong, then we feel repelled without quite knowing why. On the other hand, we feel attracted when all three drives have already undergone a certain weakening. The fact is that these three drives are continually flowing—in every person, including ourselves.

Now we have to imagine that there are countless streams like this, since one flows out of every person without being able to mingle with that of another. Quite the contrary: they all mutually repel one another. That's why we have such enormous difficulties even imagining oneness with others. The root of this behavior is the craving of ignorance.

The craving of sensuality is always looking to fulfill the wishes of our senses. We can readily discern this through mindfulness: everything is supposed to be pleasant, taste good, smell or sound good, so that the body won't have to suffer any hardship. Of course there's a positive feature to this behavior. Ultimately we are trying to shape our environment in a beautiful and pleasant fashion. The only thing wrong is when we don't realize why we're behaving this way. The drive to satisfy the senses is so strongly rooted in us that we hardly notice it anymore. Not only humans, but all living creatures, are subject to this urge. It's not just that we want something new, different, and beautiful, we want an uninterrupted supply of it. This is the great danger.

The strongest craving for satisfying the senses is undoubtedly the sexual drive, which keeps urging us on to new acts, because we hope at some point to find real fulfillment. Even when we notice what a dubious business it is, this drive doesn't get eradicated. All sensual cravings can be weakened and eventually laid aside when ignorance has been overcome. Ignorance is the opposite of wisdom, not the opposite of knowledge, because in fact we already know what's going on here. But we're so addicted to the craving of sensuality that we think of all sorts of justifications for it. We really don't want to hurt anyone, and in general the wish for sensual satisfaction is so unconscious that we don't even notice it.

Before his enlightenment the Buddha wanted to combat this drive with asceticism. He had led a life of luxury, which hadn't satisfied him. When he saw that neither luxury nor asceticism made him happy, he finally chose the Middle Way. He taught that neither a complete turning away from nor a complete turning to the senses was necessary. We may sometimes imagine that we're not caught up in everything, but that's an illusion. We give ourselves over wholly and completely to everything pleasant. Only people who have voluntarily renounced everything—save the bare necessities—can learn enduring. Enduring means being content even when we have unpleasant feelings. That isn't easy. Unpleasant feelings can be physical, when we're exposed to an unpleasant climate, have to eat something we don't like or put up with unpleasant, perhaps even dirty, lodgings. Emotional endurance is perhaps even harder. This includes putting up with verbal injuries, slanders, attacks, and the indifference of others to our own precious self. That happens to everyone at one time or another. Enduring it simply means that one is content with one's life, which naturally presupposes insight into arising and ceasing.

If one of the many demands we make should happen not to be met, we instantly conclude that an injustice has been done to us. If we want to learn to be content in every situation, we need patience and acceptance, because every one of us, even an enlightened one, is occasionally plagued by unpleasant feelings. It all depends on how we handle them. Enduring things goes so much against the grain that, rather than accept them, many people prefer to give up practicing. After sitting and meditating so long, and winning so many insights, we're now supposed to practice endurance too? That's just too much to ask.

The three subliminal cravings are, of course, closely interconnected. The craving for existence is our survival instinct. Its other side is thoughts of killing ourselves, or actual suicide attempts— the wish not to be. Both are based on the ego illusion. But what a drama, when the wish to cease existing is translated into fact! Then a new body will see to it that everything begins all over again. This happens to many people, and it's a misery to have to lose again everything that one has already gained.

The drive to exist is the strongest of our cravings—it's our vital energy. If we feel good, mentally and physically, this energy is abundant. By contrast, when we get sick, it's drastically lowered. Those who are already experienced in meditation are familiar with this feeling of surrendering and fitting into what happens. There we get an inkling of what it will be like when this drive to exist, which constantly puts pressure on us, weakens or disappears altogether. That doesn't mean that one abandons it only when the body dies—the body doesn't die that quickly! It just means that we have relieved the pressure of self-affirmation. Then we can flow along with what is, and how everything happens no longer seems quite so important. Above all it will be easier for those with some practice in enduring to let themselves be carried along.

But enduring mustn't be linked to rejection, because it's a spiritual capacity only when it is marked by contentment. Naturally this is hard and can be reached only through various stages of insight. Only when we've realized, through meditation and contemplation, that our suffering is very often triggered by our rejection of enduring, will we clearly see that all problems are traceable back to the craving to exist. Those who have seen through the ego (or "me") illusion can contentedly experience every moment because there's simply no other moment except the present one. There is a lovely Zen story about this.

A Zen master who lay dying had a little cream pastry spooned into his mouth, because people knew he liked it so much. He swallowed the tidbit, and everyone waited intently for his last words. After a while he opened his eyes again and said, with a voice already growing fainter: "That tasted good." Then he died.

Only by giving up the drive to exist and to satisfy our senses will it be possible to live a completely fulfilled life. Only when every moment becomes the most important and unique, can even momentary fulfillment be felt. Only when we no longer seek any fulfillment will we be satisfied. Everything is there for us, but we can't make it out because our mind is too full. When it becomes empty we can experience the moment in all its richness.

Every step of insight that we take leads us to wise reflection. Of course, part of practice is experience, which in turn must be reflected upon wisely.

None of us would be human beings on this earth if we weren't subject to the ego illusion, in other words to the craving of ignorance. Even little children are afflicted with it, although not so severely as adults. The Buddha explained more than once that the human level is the best for reaching enlightenment. Beyond this, the Buddha also taught that it was a great good fortune and a rarity to be born human. Those who, in addition, are mentally and physically healthy and have so much first-rate kamma that they can hear and practice the dhamma don't have even an approximate notion of how great that good fortune is.

Thus, although we're born with ignorance, which tells us we are specific individuals, nothing better can happen to us than to be here. In meditation and contemplation we have at our disposal methods by which we can transform ignorance into wisdom. In addition the Buddha has given us the gift of the Four Noble Truths that form the core of his teaching.

The first Noble Truth: Existence is dukkha.

The second Noble Truth: There is only one cause for this, craving.

The third Noble Truth: There is liberation from every sort of dukkha.

The fourth Noble Truth: The way to freedom from dukkha leads through the Eightfold Path.

If we've recognized the first two Noble Truths and know that we suffer even when most of our wishes have been fulfilled and we are living in the best conditions, we sense our lack of fulfillment. Then we'll surely set ourselves on the path of purification. This will become a matter of urgency.

The Eightfold Path consists of eight steps; but they're not to be looked upon as a ladder. They're more like circular tracks on which we practice, so that in the end we can return to the start with a completely new understanding.

The Eightfold Path is grouped into three parts, like all the Buddha's teaching: *sīla* (ethical behavior), *samādhi* (concentration), and *paññā* (wisdom). Although in many of his discourses—as in this one—the Buddha characterized ethical behavior as the foundation of his teaching, in the Eightfold Path wisdom is mentioned first. That's because it takes wisdom to see the spiritual path not as a possibility but as a necessity, and likewise for the insight that without the spiritual path we have wasted a valuable human life.

The first step is called "right understanding." In another discourse the Buddha stated that all our false understandings are based on ego. The first right understanding opens the door to the path for us and is by no means all of right understanding, which we don't acquire until we reach the end of the path. Right understanding means, first of all, the insight that material life isn't enough, and, second, that we are the owners of our kamma. We've stopped blaming others, and we know that our reactions belong to us, as all actions belong to those who perform them. It's quite clear to us that we will reap what we sow. If that doesn't quite click in our thoughts, we know that we have slid off the path. Thus we try to be constantly alert and on guard so as to quickly find our way back to the path.

That seems very laborious to many people, and it does stay that way until we become accustomed to it. Thereafter it will simply become a way of life, and a constant inner readiness to experience the new. This readiness is a necessity on the spiritual path. Our habits and those of our milieu appear so static that readiness for renewal is often disregarded. That leads to bogged-down attitudes and prejudices.

The path of wisdom includes two things: right understanding and right intention. Right intention aims at doing only good and at making the good increase in one's own heart, so that a feeling of security can grow. To be sure, this isn't done only with words or thoughts; they have to be followed up by good deeds. And the right intention of purifying ourselves means that we stop justifying and excusing ourselves. Recognize, don't blame, change! It's no use shifting the blame to others, to an evil fate or adverse circumstances. The urge toward the good becomes really strong only when urgency is acknowledged. Practicing the good is the difference between those who may have spiritual ambitions and those who really know what has to be done and then make it a reality. It's true that all those who are still subject to the ego illusion will keep getting into difficulties, but right understanding and right intention are steps of wisdom on the Eightfold Path.

QUESTIONS AND ANSWERS

Q: When does the moment of urgency come? Can one foster it, or does it come all by itself? Does it last?

A: It lasts, and it comes on the advanced path of insight, once we have left behind the fear of losing the ego. And that fear grips everyone, some powerfully, some less so. Anyone who has experienced it knows about the danger of existence. The next step leads to the urgency of practicing, because the wish for redemption from existence has gained strength. This has nothing to do with suicide, but with redemption from the ego. Urgency is based on understanding, hence it lasts. Once we have realized something, no one can take it away from us. But when we acquire a profound understanding, it will also anchor itself in us. How to foster it? By continuously observing arising and ceasing, until ceasing is so clearly recognized that everything seems to be swimming away until nothing is left behind to cling to. Then fear arises, and you have to hold on while it lasts.

Q: Is there a danger of missing enlightenment in this life?

A: No, that's not the danger. On the contrary, the danger that one sees in existence is the danger of wrongdoing, of endangering oneself and others, not being harmless, generating bad kamma, and thereby falling into bad circumstances. The prospect of possibly being extinguished at any time—which is just what we fear—is viewed as the endangering of existence. Above all, we see that this existence, if we remain without knowledge, drags one existence after another behind it, an existence that keeps bringing the same thing along with it. Existence is marked by impermanence, dukkha, and insubstantiality. So we find nothing in it that promises fulfillment. That's the danger of existence. The drive to satisfy the senses keeps filling us with hope and stimulating us to go off on a new quest. After all, it must be possible to find satisfaction somewhere. It feels good, it looks beautiful, it tastes good, it sounds good, I think of something pleasant—I must be able to find it somewhere. It's this drive for sensual satisfaction that keeps leading us to believe there must be something we can find. When you have recognized all this, the only thing left to do is practice, to liberate yourself from all of it, because explanations and words are only concepts.

Q: Is that the moment of entering the stream?
A: It's not yet the moment when urgency enters.

Q: Are greed and hatred a consequence of the sensual drive?
A: They both have the same basis, namely ignorance.

Q: So is it the sensual drive that's described as craving?
A: It depends upon what the Buddha is talking about. Here the subject is the three asavas, and sensuality is mentioned. The term "craving" is often misunderstood. Perhaps "desire" would be more accurate, the desire to satisfy the senses.

Q: I still don't understand the craving of ignorance. A drive is something that drives someone somewhere. But not to ignorance?
A: No, it's ignorance that drives. First it's sensuality that drives us; next, the wish to exist; and third, ignorance of the absolute truth. These three cravings are present in everyone and can be sensed. Sometimes we muffle them for social reasons, but then they reappear with concentrated energy. And we have problems with other people. They're so strong that we often don't recognize them, and that makes it hard to get the better of them. We can meet them only with the method of practicing, which refines and sharpens and strengthens the mind so that it can recognize the misery that arises from these

cravings. The Buddha uses his discourse to show these steps to the king. After the Buddha has spoken about understanding and explained what a great gain it represents, Ajātasattu still isn't satisfied; so the Buddha clarifies the next step, recognition of the cravings, which means an even greater gain.

14. THE LAST FRUIT
Letting Go of Cravings

ONCE WE'VE DETERMINED that we have these drives in us, it becomes clear that this isn't some sort of personal difficulty, but a universal human one. If we really grasp that fact, our expectations of ourselves and the world probably recede a bit; and our disappointments lessen accordingly, because the higher the expectation, the greater the disappointment. As soon as we've discovered the sensual drive and the drive to exist, we'll shortly come upon the fact that their root is ignorance. We're so unconscious of these cravings that it costs us a lot of effort just to find them, and most people don't take the least notice of them. Much less do they discover that these cravings are precisely what cause our problems; and they rarely get the idea of doing anything about them. Therefore we should look upon the whole chaos of the world with more acceptance and tolerance. Most of it, in fact, is based on these three cravings.

The Buddha shows us seven ways to deal with them and work on them. The first way is understanding, which means: we have to be capable of realizing that we come equipped with these drives. Then we recognize their cause and, furthermore, see that their extinction would bring us the greatest happiness. Thereafter we can set about weakening these drives through the other six ways; perhaps someday we can eradicate them completely. The four stages of knowledge, that we harbor the cravings, the cause of their presence, the happiness of extinguishing them, and the way to their extinction, are the Four Noble Truths (knowledge of dukkha, the cause of dukkha, the extinction of dukkha, and the way to get there).

But now to the six steps by which we can overcome the cravings. First, of course, is establishing that they exist. The sensual drive seduces us into always wanting to have things pleasant. We don't just want to have it pleasant—we want a whole lot more. We all have to deal non-stop with this sensual craving, because it's constantly driving us from unpleasant things to pleasant. It puts us under tremendous pressure. It's impossible to stay quiet, because we have to be continuously looking for something new. Only in meditation do we have the chance of actually finding our way to rest. Therefore the explanations of the jhānas began with the words "Secluded from sense pleasures. . . ." Otherwise we'll never find any rest.

The reason why we're so subject to these drives is ignorance. This always comes down to the fact that we haven't yet recognized the absolute truth. We mustn't understand this in the sense that we're utterly ignorant or evil. The only issue here is realizing the problematic nature of human life in general. Thus we can learn to accept that things are this way and not otherwise, and only then can we try to consciously abandon the cravings of sensuality and existence—at least during meditation, in order to get some idea of how the extinction of these drives feels. In nibbana these drives are so totally extinguished that they can never appear again. But even their momentary extinction gives us a happiness that can't be had so long as the cravings are at work in us. So long as we think, self-centeredness is also present; we know what we'd like and what we wouldn't, what we plan, hope, and want to finish off.

With his genius the Buddha has methodically shown us which paths we should follow and how we can go about it. The more we know of his teaching, the simpler it will be to follow them. By ourselves we could neither find these paths nor enter upon them. We have to rein in our sense contacts, as has already been explained. Thus, if we protect and guard them, and don't try to see, touch, smell, and hear everything, we'll limit them and renounce this or that one, and so fall into temptation far less often. Temptation is always and everywhere present in the world as long as we aren't fully enlightened; and it knocks on our door by way of our senses. The more sense contacts we have, the more we fall into temptation. We have to keep remembering that. Consciously limiting sense contacts has nothing to do with indifference, and no grand renunciations are demanded of us; but we can always practice equanimity.

Everything arises and ceases, comes and goes. The moment that something passes away we have to look for something new. The Buddha described this as "being a debtor." We keep having to take care of the unpaid bills presented by our sense contacts. We probably all pay our real bills, but we generally don't even notice the ones we run up through our senses. The first step, therefore, is limiting our sense contacts.

The second step is a question of enduring, that is, allowing unpleasant sensations in, because meanwhile the process of arising and ceasing has become clear to us. We don't need to sit there with clenched teeth and wait for the meditation period to end. We can accept that this is how it is—everything comes, everything goes. Nowhere is it written that we have a permanent claim on exclusively pleasant feelings. Since both pleasant and unpleasant things exist, we have to make do with them both. The Buddha put it this way: Things should be looked at as they really are. We should endure them, even if it isn't pleasant, and blame neither ourselves nor others for causing the unpleasantness. Thus we can accept suffering; only then are we practicing equanimity. Otherwise we feel injured, we may feel self-pity, and we can slip into depression.

We have now addressed the first step, understanding, as well as the second, reining in the senses, and the third, enduring. The fourth step is called "using." It's a strange expression that some people may not know what to do with. Fortunately the Buddha has given a precise explanation of it. It means that we humbly and gratefully use all the many blessings that flow to us without interruption. It is not self-evident that we should have a super-abundance of everything we need, that our life should be filled with comforts. We can be aware of this in humility and gratitude. Gratitude opens the heart and spills over into love. We can be grateful only for what we love. Thus the capacity for love will grow and flourish in our hearts so that one day it will no longer be limited to people. Everything that exists is worthy of love.

Hence we can love the sunrise and the sunset, a tiny beetle, a wild flower, a gnarled oak. We can always be humble and grateful for everything good in our lives, instead of focusing on what we supposedly lack.

The Buddha called the things that are indispensable for our life the "four necessities." They are food, to keep the body alive; clothing, to protect us from heat and cold; a roof over our head, so as not to be exposed to the elements; and medicine for the body when we are sick. Everything above and beyond that contributes to sensual desire. That doesn't require us to dwell in an ugly, uncared-for environment; but not every luxury has to be there, only what is really "used." There's a great difference between what's necessary and what one would like to have. Those who rigorously comply with this rule will be able to clear out at least half of their belongings. Of course, that doesn't do anyone any good unless somebody else can use those things. On the other hand, it's also liberating when we get rid of things that really just weigh us down, since they demand permanent care. The less we drag around with us, the easier it is to recognize the truth.

Next comes a very interesting step, "avoiding." The Buddha said that unpleasant, unsatisfactory, and irritating situations and persons should be avoided. If we are constantly exposed to people and things that rub us the wrong way, we react in a way that's not beneficial to our spiritual growth. Thus we have to learn to recognize when our spiritual growth is called into question. The Buddha directs us to avoid bad friends because we are so easy to influence. We believe in a person's goodness until someone gives a bad report about him or her. Then we believe that. Unfortunately we're generally inclined to believe the bad, because it makes us look better ourselves—we couldn't be as bad as that person!

The Buddha said the following about a bad friend: A person who is ill-natured in personal relations has a destructive effect. He doesn't build up, he tears down. In addition, a bad friend is miserly, and not only with material things but also with his time. When his help is necessary, he never has time, because he is intent on his own advantage. This miserliness is also shown by his demanding more than he is willing to give. All these qualities are a clear warning for us not to fall into such errors ourselves. We can and should examine ourselves and our behavior. Recognize, don't blame, change! If we have discovered that we're stingy and we chide ourselves for this, we have already loaded ourselves with two bits of dukkha. A further characteristic of the bad friend is speaking negatively about us behind our back. This we especially have to avoid, which unfortunately doesn't prevent it from happening to everyone. People have spoken ill even of the Buddha and Jesus. So it's no wonder that this sort of thing happens to us as well.

But we can take care that we ourselves don't spread evil about others. A bad friend often fulfills her duties to us only because there might be negative consequences if she refused. On this point the Buddha explained that fear and shame are the guardians of the world. Meanwhile we know that nature furnishes us with good and bad qualities. Fear of blame and having to be ashamed often holds us back from doing wrong. That isn't wrong in itself, but it's still the lowest level of being good. If fear and shame were lost, we would become criminals. When a whole country is gripped by psychosis and loses its fear and shame, we have war. Once fear and shame have won back their normal place, at least we're no longer living in chaos. Thus shame and fear are the guardians of rational behavior. But if someone does her duty only out of fear and shame, we cannot call her a friend. Friends do their duty out of love and inclination.

Likewise a bad friend is someone who flatters us and spreads evil about us behind our back. So it's appropriate to mistrust every kind of flattery; it points to a person who is untruthful and doesn't stand up for his convictions. If we can sincerely affirm that we ourselves don't act that way, we'll get a sense of security. But we have to be very careful that we don't have this sort of person in our circle of friends, because he or she will only harm us. Now, however, we see our milieu as a mirror image of what we bear within us. If we don't have such unpleasant characteristics ourselves, it will be very hard to recognize them in others. But if they do catch our eye, we'll have to admit that we once had them or still have them. The result of such recognition must not in any case be hatred. With hatred we harm no one so much as ourselves.

So if we realize that someone is not a good friend, we should avoid him and all situations in which he might harm us, but nevertheless continue to hold him in our hearts with love. We don't necessarily have to spend time with him, because we all have only a limited amount of it. We have twenty-four hours a day, of which we spend six to eight sleeping; in addition we have to work to earn a living. Hence our time has to be wisely budgeted. This is what the Buddha called "wise reflection." Being amiably disposed to a bad friend means that despite everything we wish only good things for her, summon up compassion for her, and help her when she asks for it and can accept the help. But we're on guard against situations where she could harm us. It's rather complicated!

Of course, the Buddha also described the good friend, whom we treat carefully and whom we should emulate. Through wise reflection one can put one's life on a harmonious basis and recognize the deeper truths. A good friend needs no excuses, for example, that she had no time to help us. She protects our possessions, is helpful, and rejoices at our welfare. She entrusts her secrets to us and keeps ours. Only someone with whom we can speak heart to heart is a real friend. With him or her we discuss what really moves us. He gives good advice, is generous, frank, confident, and loyal. Friends help one another by always sticking to the truth. In no way does that mean constant criticism. Finding out the reasons for another's difficulties and trying to help out—that is truth. He or she is no fair-weather friend, but sticks with us through thick and thin. He prevents others from speaking ill about his friend and himself speaks only good of him. Finding that sort of friend is difficult and rare. But if you get one, he or she must be treated like a jewel.

In general, interpersonal relations are marked by vanity and selfishness. But where two people mean well by one another and the relationship isn't used for one's own advantage, we'll find this mutual opening of the heart. It's clear that we have to be a good friend ourselves in order to have good friends of our own. It's impossible to experience something that hasn't already sent down roots in us. Thus the Buddha demands that we avoid a bad environment and seek a good one.

The next point is "putting aside." This means the four great efforts: (1) to not allow an unwholesome thought to arise that has not yet arisen; (2) to not allow an unwholesome thought that has arisen to continue; (3) to a let a wholesome thought arise that has not yet arisen; (4) to continue a wholesome thought that has already arisen. In doing so we keep giving our mind the option of changing for the better. Letting go is much harder than replacing. The moment something is dropped, that creates a sort of vacuum; and if we don't watch out, it gets filled immediately with the very thing we wanted to let go of. But if we deliberately replace it, we at least save the moment.

This rescue operation is all the easier, the more the mind has been strengthened through concentration. Just as out on the ocean waves we need strength to save ourselves from drowning, we need the strength of the one-pointed mind to save us from unwholesome thoughts. And so the Buddha continuously recommended mindfulness to protect us at the very onset of negativity. Control of thoughts helps us to de-energize our cravings. If we don't recognize hatred and greed in time, we nourish the cravings of sensuality and existence, which hold us fast in the cycle of worldly events. The stronger these cravings are, the less we can feel our inner happiness and spiritual bliss. Replacing unwholesome thoughts is like standing on a cliff, from which we could slide down at the slightest unmindfulness. To be sure, this sliding would affect only our body. But our thoughts and our mind are what move us. The body only follows after, because it has no choice. So it's our job to protect not the body, but the mind, from sliding downhill. To do that we have to continuously remind ourselves of the four great efforts.

The seventh point is called "unfolding." Here we are dealing with the seven factors that lead to enlightenment and that once again begin with mindfulness. It may sound troublesome and difficult to always be mindful, to develop the good, and avoid evil, but it's exactly the opposite. It imparts interest and a sense of having accomplished something; and it protects the mind from laziness and sleepiness. Next comes the examination of all phenomena that exist in the universe with a view to their impermanence, their dukkha, and their insubstantiality. The third factor is willpower. The four next factors are the meditative absorptions: rapture, calm, concentration, and equanimity. As a factor of enlightenment, equanimity has already been so internalized through understanding that it's firmly rooted.

These are the seven factors of enlightenment, which consist in calm and understanding. We have to exercise and perfect both of these, but which one succeeds first will depend on how the individual practices. Men and women with highly analytical minds must, to some degree, reach understanding before calm enters in. Here there are no value judgments; what's important is regular practice and acceptance of what happens. With the seven factors of enlightenment, understanding is mentioned first, and then come the stages of the serenity meditation.

The seven steps are there to strengthen our self-knowledge and to diminish our cravings. We can't help ourselves and heal ourselves until we know what's in our heart. For example, if we consult a doctor because we have pain, as a matter of course we expect him to recognize immediately which organ is causing us problems. And then, naturally, he has to prescribe something to give us immediate relief; otherwise we'll never go back to him. The Buddha was sometimes called "the great physician" and dhamma "the purest medicine." Although the Buddha has provided a diagnosis of our sufferings and has also prescribed the remedy, he nonetheless taught that we have to heal ourselves and recognize the diagnosis as correct. Knowledge of the diagnosis and the remedy are of no use unless we apply them. We can compare this to a medicine that we admire but refuse to swallow. We won't get the Buddha's medicine anywhere else; and it does no good to try to extract from it certain components that we believe will be helpful. The medicine that the Buddha recommends is an integral formula, and only works when it's taken that way.

On the other hand, it's such a radical and comprehensive medicine that it can't be swallowed all at once. It must be taken spoonful by spoonful. Each one, however, contains all the components and can lead to our feeling better. To be really cured requires the whole bottle with all the ingredients. But if we gradually find ourselves feeling better, and we notice that the medicine helps, we'll continue to take it. Unfortunately there is a widespread bad habit of picking and choosing from the medicine whatever strikes us as convenient. And there are so many ways of justifying this: it takes too much time . . . after all, I'm no Buddhist . . . my friends don't like it . . . and so on. But though this medicine sometimes doesn't taste good at all (it contains no sweeteners), it has to be taken in its entirety and to the end in order to effect a cure. If, besides, we happen to find the packaging beautiful, that will help us to love the medicine that makes our healing easier.

QUESTIONS AND ANSWERS

Q: I'd like to ask something about impermanence. On this point the thought of loving-kindness occurred to me. Is that impermanent too?

A: In the universal, infinite consciousness everything exists that has ever become conscious. But everything has the quality of coming together or coming into being and falling apart or disintegrating. This holds true for every thought and every perception. But final decay and total impermanence no longer have any connection to infinite consciousness. Here in the relative world, we have only disintegration, whereas in infinite consciousness everything exists that ever was. But that too has the quality of coming and going.

Q: I can't imagine loving-kindness and equanimity as changeable. If it were changeable, then it would no longer be loving-kindness.

A: That's a relative truth. Relatively speaking, one can say that loving-kindness is always included in infinite consciousness, and that there are people who always feel loving-kindness. But absolutely speaking, there is nothing that doesn't come together and fall apart—including the entire universe. Even that contracts and collapses. The same thing is true of all states of consciousness. It's not a question of an either/or, but of a both/and. You can also say that loving-kindness always exists, but nothing exists on an absolute basis.

Q: What is *sangha*?

A: Many people believe that all those who sit down on a meditation cushion are the sangha. That's definitely one meaning of the word. In translation *sangha* means "community," and in Buddhism it refers to monks and nuns. In the formula of taking refuge, *sangha* means the Enlightened Ones. Of course we wish to take refuge with the enlightened, because this highest ideal offers real protection.

Q: How should I understand the cravings in terms of practice?

A: We should see whether we can find the cravings in us. There is a big difference between intellectual or academic knowledge and practice. The Buddha recommended both. If there is no study and understanding, the Buddha's teachings remain foreign to us. If practice is missing, then we can't internalize the real meaning.

With words alone we can only develop a concept, which always remains merely static. By contrast, practice is something that flows and continuously provokes new things until we reach the end, enlightenment. The three cravings are in principle only words. We have to carefully examine whether they are actually there. It's extraordinarily interesting to ferret them out. This instinctive force keeps leading us down the wrong paths. If we can finally compel it to halt at some point—even if just briefly—we'll be able to set off in a new direction. These findings will then be felt as a quality of the heart, and as something altogether different from anything we have hitherto experienced.

15 THE EIGHTFOLD PATH
Morality and Concentration

JUST AS WE CAN RECOGNIZE the existence of the cravings
and what triggers them, and just as we can feel their extinction
as a great blessing, so the Eightfold Path leads us to recognize
dukkha. The extinguishing of dukkha is the greatest blessing of
all, and the Buddha has explained eight steps to attain it. But
before we can take the first step, we must have grasped our own
dukkha. This dukkha is by no means a human problem that
shows up, causes problems, and then at some point or other is
solved or disappears of its own accord. We have to recognize that
dukkha is part of the foundation of our existence. So long as we
haven't clearly seen that, there is no reason to follow the path.

Most people admit that they have dukkha, and each one finds
some reason or other for it. But if it's limited to a specific problem, for example, with our partner, or with meditation, or something like that, then we'll simply take pains to get rid of this one
problem—or two or three of them (there's always a large selec-
tion: a lack of self-confidence, of loving-kindness, tolerance, and
so on). But that's not what the Buddha meant—that's not the
path to freedom. At issue here is a universal problem that has
nothing to do with personal difficulties. Existence in itself is dukkha, independent of our capacities or incapacities. Dukkha is
completely impersonal and applies to every existence.

Because we sense dukkha, but don't clearly recognize its primordial cause, we try to get satisfaction through the sensual desires. But even then, when over the course of the years we have
drastically cut back on our expectations, we won't find complete
satisfaction and fulfillment. So we have no alternative but to take
the first step and accept impermanence. This gives us access to
the understanding of dukkha. Impermanence and constant

change cause suffering so long as we don't wholly and completely consent to it. With this acceptance it becomes possible to enter upon the path to the extinction of dukkha full of energy and devotion.

Dukkha emerges from the fact that everything that moves causes friction. If we look closely, we can discern that in our mental formations. And even if we don't notice it, in any case we find that even the best meditation passes away. Nothing is permanent. Even if we seek very mindfully, we'll find nothing that lasts; and so we may discover that this eternal passing away brings about dukkha. One minute things are going well—the next minute they're not. That's the up-and-down of life. We have to submit to it in order to realize that our life is simply subject to dukkha. Having accepted that, we no longer need to suffer from it. We have suffered before only because we always wanted to get rid of every kind of unpleasantness—in other words: dukkha—as fast as possible. We don't want to feel any discomfort, so it has to be driven away as urgently as possible. And this very resistance prevents us from going with the flow, which is where the pain of opposition arises. Only moving with the flow makes everything simple and easy.

So we have to let go and follow the Eightfold Path, which consists of three parts. The first part relates to wisdom, the next concerns moral behavior. There is no true spiritual doctrine and no religion that is not based upon purified behavior. This is simply because morally irreproachable behavior relieves our own lives and those of our fellow men and women. Those who do less bumping cause less pain to themselves and others.

If we purify our behavior, which contains hatred and craving, we can move forward. The three steps of the second part of the path are: right speech, right action, right livelihood. The call for right speech is double-edged, because polite speech isn't always truthful. It can be thoroughly manipulative or suggestive, trying to head the other person in a specific direction. That's not right speech, because it's not truthful. And our speech should always be concerned with the unvarnished truth. No half-truths or what we think the listener can cope with—no, it has to be the whole truth. We don't need to absolutely blurt things out; but if we do speak up, we have to stand by what we've recognized as right. Furthermore, we have to strive to pass on the truth from heart to heart and not from head to head. A dialogue is worthwhile only when it's carried out in this light.

Of course, we have to earn money to support ourselves and we have to perform bureaucratic tasks. So there's no way to avoid some purely cerebral conversation; but even then "heart-to-heart language" is far more effective. After all, we're still talking with a person who has a heart too. In any case we can't give anything of ourselves that isn't colored by our intellect. If besides that our speech also contains cordial warmth, then we're talking the right language and we feel refreshed ourselves. And in this language there are no untruths. Only those who don't speak frankly can speak untruthfully. If we say what we feel, we make it possible for our interlocutor to express what he or she feels. In that case differences of opinion are possible, but not conflict.

The first discourse that the Buddha delivered to his son Rahula (whose name, by the way, means "fetter"), when the boy was seven years old, deals with lying. The Buddha left his palace and family on the day his son was born, to begin his search for the path leading out of human dukkha. He promised to return when he had discovered this path. When he did return, the mother of little Rahula sent the boy to his father to demand his inheritance. Rahula did as he was told, although he didn't even know what an inheritance was. So the Buddha delivered his first discourse to Rahula, the most precious legacy that he could have left his son.

The Buddha took a ladle and filled it with water. He asked his son: "What do you see here?" "A ladle full of water" was the child's answer. Then the Buddha spilled out the water and asked: "And what do you see now?" "Now the ladle is empty," the boy responded. The Buddha then explained that the life of a liar was as empty as this ladle. He twisted the ladle around and said: "That is how twisted the life of a human being is who lies." Then he scooped up a little water with the ladle and explained that that was how one should practice: always taking up a little until the ladle was filled. And when it was full, it symbolized a person full of happiness and without lies. Then the Buddha took an empty can and showed it to Rahula: "What's in there?" he asked. "Nothing at all," the child replied. The Buddha said: "Fill this can with water." Rahula did so; the Buddha took it, turned it upside down, and all the water ran out. Just so, the Buddha explained, all goodness flows away from a person who lies. In this way he tried to explain that lies affect people in such a way that all good is lost.

Then he showed Rahula a mirror and asked: "What is that?" Rahula answered that it was a mirror, whereupon the Buddha wanted to know: "What is a mirror good for?" The boy answered that he could see himself in it. The Buddha then explained that a mirror was very important, because if a person could look at himself in it, he could see whether he had lied or not. Granted, the Buddha said that to a seven-year-old; but it's every bit as true for us. Lies, the Buddha explains in one of his discourses, aren't just the opposite of the truth. Even when we tell only half the truth about something or pass over something in silence, it's a lie. Often we gloss over something to make it look better. Who doesn't keep quiet about something now and then, so as not to look like a complete idiot? Or we say only what we hope to get some advantage from. All that is not the complete truth. Whatever doesn't come from the heart can easily be defective.

The Buddha addressed the subject of right speech in detail. Right speech is one of the thirty-eight great blessings, because a person who sticks to the truth will never suffer from regret. An impulsive statement can lead to our losing a friend. Interpersonal relations are built on language and the feelings that are behind it. Hence the closer one is to his or her own feelings, the closer one is to those of others. There is a wonderful German proverb: "Lies have short legs." Obviously short legs don't carry us as far as long ones. Lies lack the power of conviction. Even if they aren't immediately exposed, they leave no inspiration behind them. Hence in our speech we mostly have to rely on our feelings and, over and above that, to use language that is neither impolite nor unfriendly nor downright nasty. Still, the choice of words is far from being the most important thing. When we're talking to a person who is perfectly aware that we don't like him or her, we can deliver the worst insults with the politest words. On the other hand, we can say something harsh to a person who is convinced of our love, and he or she won't hold it against us. The feelings behind the word are understood precisely by our conversation partner.

So we should carefully hold out a mirror before ourselves while we listen to what we are saying. If our speech becomes angry, then we have to take a deep breath and consider that the person who has angered us did so only out of his own dukkha. If he were happy, he wouldn't have had to say something provoking, and in the long run we only harm ourselves when we get angry. So anger has to be replaced with compassion. We have a choice. We can react, or we can let it be, for our own good and that of the other. Right speech has no need of special rhetorical skills.

Of course, we have to weigh our words, especially when we talk about dhamma. We have to strive for wise reflection, for insight, and for precision in our mode of expression, because every person has a different notion of every term. Even when the same language is being spoken, often enough there are misunderstandings. Right speech arises out of right thoughts, and if the heart joins in the conversation, the choice of words won't be hard.

The next step consists in right actions. The four precepts that do not refer to speech lay down the boundaries: (1) do not kill, (2) do not steal, (3) do not commit any sexual misconduct, and (4) do not take any drugs or intoxicating drinks. Right action is based on the quite simple foundation of not harming anyone by what we do. Our action should rather be helpful and should benefit ourselves and others. Fundamentally there are countless persons who would gladly help in some way or another, but they don't know how to go about it. We first have to have developed helpful capacities before we can provide any help.

Thus we have a progressive experience. First thought, then speech, and finally action. We have to know that with our thoughts we cause the least kamma, with speech a medium amount, and finally with our actions the most.

Now, of course, an action that's over and done with is very hard to change or reverse. A thought, on the other hand, is much easier to change; it disappears all by itself, without our doing anything. Since we generally believe our thoughts, we have to begin with purification; and we shouldn't forget that the creation of kamma begins with thought. Everything negative, without exception, generates negative kamma. Thus, if we clean house with our thoughts and no longer admit negativity, it's hardly possible for something to go wrong with our speech and actions. Those who have cleaned up their thoughts will also have order in other realms of life. Those who don't confront this fundamental task will have a hard time giving a positive shape to speech and action, so as to bring harmony into their own lives and those of their fellow humans.

Right livelihood is part of the foundation of the spiritual conduct of one's life, and so it shouldn't come into conflict with the five precepts: no killing, no stealing, no sexual misconduct, no wrong speech, no alcohol or drugs. Right livelihood helps in many ways: we don't need to regret anything, and we don't develop any guilt feelings. We don't get together with people whose speech and action are misdirected and who have no interest in a spiritual life. Right livelihood spares us such difficulties. Should we harbor doubts as to whether our livelihood is appropriate for a spiritual life, we need only compare our everyday actions with the five precepts to see whether any of them is being violated.

An important component of wise reflection is also the guarding or protecting of our own happiness. How do we do that? It's best to write down what we consider happiness, and then consider what we should do or avoid to protect it.

The third part of the Eightfold Path, which is concerned with training the mind, consists in turn of three steps, namely: right effort, right mindfulness, and right concentration. It immediately becomes clear that mindfulness and concentration aren't one and the same. Mindfulness leads to concentration, which we need for meditation. The more we practice mindfulness in our everyday life, the easier we'll find meditation.

Right effort primarily embraces the four great efforts of the mind, to deal rightly with wholesome and unwholesome thoughts (see chapter 14). Right effort is also knowing how we are investing our energy, whether we are wasting it in sensual satisfaction or directing it on the right track. This is the most important consideration for me: how do I spend my time? Right effort is being made when we use our time for meditation and contemplation.

The jhānas are states of consciousness toward which we make strides by concentrating on our breath. Mindfulness focused on breathing in and out leads us to right concentration—to composure, where we gather all the mind's energies at one point. If we have collected all these energies together, they're naturally much stronger than if they were scattered far and wide. Having undertaken all the steps that belong to the Eightfold Path, we then return to the first step—to right understanding—and now the picture we have of ourselves has changed. Since we are the center of our life, we have to proceed from our center. Only from within do we come to the truth. The steps on the Eightfold Path lead to our purification. Effort, mindfulness, and the jhānas make it clear to us that up to now we have had a completely illusory image of ourselves. The recognition of dukkha, of coming into being and passing away, and the states of consciousness in the jhānas show us that there is no individuality in any of us. When we internalize that, we are breaking new ground. Individuality is precisely what's forever causing us great difficulties. If we're willing to look at ourselves without individuality, dukkha will lose all its power over us. Everyone has the possibility of getting rid of dukkha once and for all; there simply has to be the will to do so.

On a forest walk with his monks the Buddha once bent down and picked up a few dried leaves. He showed them to the monks and asked them where more leaves were to be seen, in his hand or on the trees. The monks answered that obviously there were far more leaves on the trees. Then the Buddha said: "The difference between what I know and what I have taught you is just as great as that between the number of the leaves on the trees and the number of leaves in my hand. But what I have taught you, which is comparable to the leaves in my hand, is enough for your enlightenment. I have also always taught with an open hand, that is, I have never made a mystery of anything. All that you know now is enough for enlightenment."

Hence on many statues of the Buddha one can find a *mudra* (hand gesture), the open left hand. This means no closed fist, in other words, no mysteries. Everything is open and accessible to everyone. In the Buddha's teaching nothing is withheld. Every intelligent person who is willing to practice will find open explanations. The only thing needed is time, willpower, and the knowledge of dukkha. The Buddha said of himself: "I teach only one thing: dukkha, and the end of dukkha."

QUESTIONS AND ANSWERS

Q: In the precepts the Buddha says that one shouldn't kill any living creature. On the other hand, needy persons are supposed to accept with gratitude whatever they get. Does that mean they may accept only vegetarian food, or doesn't that have anything to do with it?

A: That really has nothing at all to do with this rule. One should eat what one gets, but one shouldn't kill. This question keeps coming up. Monks and nuns are supposed to be humble and gratefully accept what they're given. Thus in the monastery the cuisine is vegetarian, but outside it there's no possibility of choice.

Q: That's the case in monasteries, because nobody's allowed to slaughter an animal.

A: Naturally no one would do that in a monastery; but laypeople bring whatever occurs to them, and it's accepted with thanks. The Buddha said very clearly that his teaching was not to be a religion about eating, because even back then there were enough of them. The "sacred cow" was already familiar to the Hindus, and it caused enormous anger. Millions of people have been killed because of differences of opinion about food. A fanatical view about whether beef or pork should be eaten has already triggered catastrophes. The Buddha strictly rejected every kind of fanaticism, since such things are merely a kind of clinging.

Q: So I shouldn't learn the trade of a butcher?
A: No—under no circumstances.

Q: I have a practical problem. How do I get rid of the mosquitoes in my bedroom?
A: In Sri Lanka the problem is much worse!

Q: Do we really have to respect even bugs?
A: Yes, of course! Killing is killing, and living creatures are still living creatures. When this law is broken, the responsibility always lies with the perpetrator. We have to bear the consequences of what we do.

Q: Does the eighth step of the Eightfold Path refer to the jhānas?
A: Concentration always refers to the jhānas, because the whole meditation leads in that direction.

Q: A question about truth: on the one hand, you're supposed to tell the whole truth; on the other hand, you're supposed to keep it to yourself if the truth isn't helpful.
A: If you know a truth that would cause injury, and the other person would suffer from this knowledge, you shouldn't injure the other person.

Q: Then unvarnished truth is a truth that doesn't hurt somebody?
A: That's correct. But the manner and style of dealing with the truth are important. This certainly doesn't mean that the

truth should be manipulated or held back. It just has to be lovingly imparted so that no one gets hurt.

Q: Earlier you said that an open heart is a prerequisite for loving action. But quite often there are situations where one person has an open heart, and the other person doesn't.

A: That does happen frequently, and that's why interpersonal relations are difficult. They only work well when there's a heart-to-heart connection. You can try establishing this sort of connection as long as possible. And if it absolutely won't work, only one thing helps: establish distance lovingly, in order to protect yourself. Of course, all interpersonal relations are continuously flowing and changing, but the Buddha's general rules point in this direction.

16. DISENCHANTMENT AND FREEDOM FROM CRAVING

THE DISCOURSE THAT THE BUDDHA delivered to King Ajātasattu revolves around the progressive growth that begins with everyday behavior and ends in enlightenment. Most of the Buddha's discourses had this form. There are, admittedly, some in which a certain maturity is presupposed. There he was probably speaking to people who had already been practicing for some time; but here the king was an absolute novice. So the Buddha began with the beginning, by explaining moral behavior, restraining the senses, mindfulness, and contentment, then the jhānas and the understanding that results from them, up to the moment when fear makes its appearance, when the danger, and with it the urgency of practicing, is recognized and the wish for release arises.

It doesn't make any difference where exactly on the path we find ourselves. According to the Buddha, the only important thing is to be aware of the whole path, in order to know its goal and direction. This may be compared to an orientation map on which various directions and points of reference are indicated, with a red dot saying "You are here." A person who doesn't know where he or she is standing can't possibly know in what direction he or she has to go. Unfortunately, on the spiritual path there are no such clearly marked road signs. But sincerity about ourselves helps us to recognize whether we feel anger and craving or peace and calm; and whether we have already internalized impermanence so much that the ego has lost a little of its seeming solidity. It doesn't matter where we are on the path: we have to know about this without disappointment and without blame; otherwise all our practice will be blocked. Both those who already imagine that they are in the higher regions and those who think themselves utterly incapable of it, lack this possibility of orientation. The inner self-examination—who, where, and how we are—has to be undertaken quite objectively, without any confirmation from outside.

We have already experienced in our daily lives many things that are a part of the purification process, because we know intuitively that peace is to be found only when purity of mind and heart has been acquired. Naturally we've made many mistakes, but now that we have clear guidelines, we can take to the path with more concentration and trust. If we've come to a point where we still have the wish for release, then by definition we're still not perfectly happy; because desirelessness happens only in the jhāna of meditation or to an enlightened person. And every meditation comes to an end, and with it the sensation of happiness. But that's exactly what drives us on to practice with perseverance and discipline.

True, meditation is the most important means on the way, but it's only a means. Everything further is subject to wise reflection and recognition. Hence, the next step is dedicated to the three distinguishing features of existence, of which we examine one in particular. Quite often those who are practicing busy themselves with the non-self, with anatta. Of course, it could also be dukkha to which we turn at this stage. Meanwhile dukkha has become clear to us, because we have noted that there is nothing that can really leave us satisfied, and because we have accepted the constant nature of change. We have seen coming into being and passing away and lived through the fear that we can't keep everything our heart is attached to. Thus, the wish is born to free ourselves from this fatal cycle. The examination of the "non-self" doesn't take place on an intellectual, logical plane. Rather it's an attempt to journey deep into ourselves, to recognize the "me."

Generally the "me," the ego, is so strong that every discovery is impeded. It wishes to assert itself, because the ego wants power. It wants to live, even beyond death. When it loses power, which happens very seldom, we have the possibility of objectively examining our makeup, our body and mind. Now the mind can test what is actually sitting there and trying to meditate. Here we have to direct our mind to our sensations. But who is actually doing the directing? And what are the feelings? In a person who is unpracticed in meditation, feeling is largely shaped by the ego. That's why it usually saddles us with a great deal of unrest and a certain heaviness.

Only in the jhānas is calm in charge. But we can't stay in it permanently, and just to get this far calls for a great deal of concentration. Many external conditions are also required. First of all, we need time to meditate and, beyond that, a quiet place and freedom from disturbance. Another extremely important thing is health, for without it we cannot persevere in sitting. Thus, to be able to meditate and, yet more, to reach the jhānas we are dependent on many factors. So a vast number of external things— noises and other circumstances—can disturb us and make us wholly incapable of meditation. We become angry because we are dependent on concrete conditions. Unfortunately we can't always pick and choose them, because, like everything else, they are the results of causes. This shows that nothing subject to conditions can ever be completely satisfying.

The Buddha was a genius at analysis, and probably the greatest psychologist of all time. Of course, there are also other spiritual disciplines that have recognized fundamental truths and still teach them today. The difference lies in the clarity and the practical directives. The Buddha explains even the smallest aspect in meticulous detail, so that his teaching is really accessible to everyone. Perhaps we weren't initially so interested in Buddhist teaching. We may have started meditating only because we wanted to bring a little calm into our lives. Then through meditation we got into the examination of the self—the ego—and that spurred our curiosity. If we made a serious start at sincerely observing ourselves and our motivation, we had to admit that our character wasn't as snow-white as we had always thought. We recognize the excuses and justifications that we are forever coming up with. Perhaps we even realize that our whole life up to now has been built on conditions over which we have little or no control.

First, there are the conditions that we're familiar with from our previous experiences: if you love me, you have to admire, protect, and understand me; otherwise I can't love you back. If you give me security, I'll give you trust, and so forth. But these external circumstances are unreliable and hence unsatisfactory. And because we can never completely determine them, we're insecure and restless. Our moods too are dependent on external conditions and hence unreliable, just like our trains of thought. Everything is constantly melting away, so we stand in the universe without any support; and we try to find security in either unreachable wishes or material objects. But both these possibilities for evasion are subject to decay, like everything else in and around us; hence they contribute to our insecurity and anxiousness. We can't bear this insecurity until we really accept it. Then it loses its terror, and we need expend no further energy.

This step is called disenchantment, and it turns out to be the first step that transcends the world. When this disenchantment takes place, we have already left the material world a little bit behind us. We have realized how much of the colorful glitter is nothing but fool's gold. We know that almost everything can be bought. But what is a human heart worth when it's paid for with money? It can never be a more than a substitute. When we notice that, we become disenchanted with this world. We have a stronger desire for liberation and release, for the absolute truth and reality that can lead us back to the source of being. The path there is illustrated by a story from the life of the Buddha.

After Prince Siddhartha left the palace of his father and learned the jhānas from two teachers, he turned to asceticism, but it failed to bring him to his goal. Then he went to Bodh-gaya and sat under a tree to meditate, because he wanted at all costs to find the answer to dukkha. This particular tree was revered by the local people because it was supposed to be inhabited by a *deva*, a tree spirit that helped women who couldn't have children.

Near the tree lived a woman named Sujata, who had begged the deva to help her conceive. And in fact nine months later this woman did bear a child. She had wanted to make a large sacrificial offering, should her wish to have a child be fulfilled. But after the child was born, Sujata had so many duties to attend to that she neglected to keep her promise. So one day she sent her housemaid to the tree to prepare a ceremony. When the maid got to the tree, the Buddha was sitting there; and she assumed that he was the deva of the tree. She told him: "My mistress wants to present the offering she promised. So I beg you, stay here, we're just about to do it." Then she ran to her mistress and told her that the tree spirit was sitting there in visible form. Sujata milked a hundred cows and gave this milk to fifty cows to drink. Then she milked fifty cows and gave the milk to twenty cows to drink. Then she milked twenty cows and gave their milk to a single cow. When she had milked this last cow, she got pure cream. She cooked a rice pudding with it, a food that to this day is offered to monks and nuns on solemn occasions in Sri Lanka. Sujata filled a large golden bowl with the rice pudding and brought it to the tree where the Buddha was meditating. He took the bowl and ate the rice. When the bowl was empty, Sujata said: "Please keep this bowl; it is my thanks for hearing my plea for a child." The Buddha, who at this point was still a bodhisattva, took the bowl and threw it into the river. He said: "If this bowl floats down the stream, I will not be enlightened. But if it floats upstream, I will achieve enlightenment." The bowl must have floated upstream, because the Buddha is in fact the Enlightened One.

This story has a special meaning for us: those who swim with the current have it easy, because the current helps, and most people do exactly that. However, in the end one lands in the mud of the river mouth   like everyone else. Along the way there is most likely just one problem: how to keep your head above water. Those who swim against the current naturally have a much harder time of it. One really has to exert oneself. True, there isn't a lot of traffic in this direction, but those who are headed downstream will probably try to make it clear by their shouts that we're going in the wrong direction. Of course, at this point it will be hard to maintain our confidence. Still, the goal will repay all the effort, for we will come to the source of being, which is clean and pure and makes us happy. But there can be absolutely no doubt that it's much harder to swim against the current. It develops muscles that didn't even exist. The actual

difficulty, however, is that we have to buck popular opinion—
and above all, our own instincts—in swimming against the current.

In fact the longer we're on the spiritual path, the stronger we
get. When we defend ourselves against our instincts and im-
pulses, we are fighting against the three poisons or negative
drives of greed, hatred, and delusion. If we have done that for
some time, we become disenchanted, realizing that the whole
thing is just a play, that the world is just a stage. At the end
of each performance, the curtain falls. The body dies. And it
immediately rises again, for the mind moves on to a new play.
It's a theater without end, with the world and the universe as the
scenery. Once we've gotten far enough to recognize this, we take
the next step, freedom from craving (*viraga*).

To experience freedom from craving, the three negative drives
must have been forced into the background. In addition we must,
of course, have known them in all their strength. Astonishingly,
the positives can block our path as well as the negatives. We can
hold out in negativity by defending ourselves and not letting anything approach us, or we can open up and try to get as much as
possible. In both cases the ego is at center stage. Hence exercising
and acquiring concentration is crucial. It's not so much a question
of actually having done all the jhānas, though that would be extremely helpful, but simply of the mind's being able to enter the
depths. That's where the Buddha's teaching is leading us. Enlightenment can take place only in the depths, and for that the
mind must come to rest and be able to step aside. The continuous
activity of the mind is responsible for this non-stop theater,
where something always has to be going on or else the audience
will get restless. In all this we are at once directors, actors, and
spectators. We make up the whole play by ourselves.

If we have managed to concentrate our mind, then it's time
to explore the qualities of the universe. What's needed here is
objectivity, not the ego anymore, because as long as the "me" is
still haunting the scene, no depth perspective is possible. This
personality, which keeps us so busy, is the number one trouble-
maker. Of course, we can't grasp this until we have experienced

the jhānas, because then we notice that at the time there wasn't anything there to make trouble. Realizing this is enormously helpful for putting an end to the ubiquitous cult of personality. To get that far, you need willpower, but understanding is far more important. With violence we can't get anywhere: everything takes time. Every step, even the smallest, brings us further along. The Buddha has given us a comparison for this: when we stand on the shore of the ocean and go into the water, first our feet get wet. After a few steps the water comes up to our knees. After some more steps the water reaches our chest and our shoulders, and at last we are completely swallowed by the sea.

Through the jhānas we learn that everything built up on conditions can never fully satisfy us. The body consists of conditions; it is composed of individual parts, and every single part must function, or the body will be incapable of life. Health is a prerequisite for the mind too, or else it can't work perfectly. The meditative mind is searching for the primordial ground of being. We're looking for what is independent of all conditions and hence without any unrest. We understand the words, but keep experiencing the opposite of what we're really longing for. Our mind, when it has reached the jhānas, is seeking what's inalterable, what lasts, and what can be found only through meditation.

It's not all that simple to internalize the process of disenchantment, because the world keeps speaking to us through our senses. Every flower shows us how beautiful it is, and so we forget all too easily to observe its passing away: we're rather more interested in its fresh coming into being. Precisely because the world keeps touching us through our senses, disenchantment constitutes a giant step toward handling the negative instincts.

This may be elucidated by a story set in India around the time of the Buddha. A married couple had quarreled furiously, and since by now this was a frequent occurrence, the wife decided to leave her husband while he was away at work. She dressed in her best saris, one on top of the other, put on all her gold jewelry, and hurried off. When her husband came home after work, the quarrel had been causing him great pain for some time; but now his wife was gone, and he couldn't make peace with her. Since her best saris and all her gold jewelry were missing, he knew that she meant to leave him. He rushed out to look for her, but couldn't find her, because she had gotten a big head start. On the street he met a monk who was going in the direction that his wife had probably taken, so he asked him: "Your Reverence, did you meet a woman wearing beautiful saris, with a lot of gold jewelry and long black hair?" The monk answered: "I saw a set of teeth hurry past." The monk was so practiced in restraining his senses that he had seen neither beautiful dresses nor jewelry nor even a woman. He had seen only a set of teeth.

This story offers a precise illustration of disenchantment. If we ourselves haven't gotten that far, we have to work on our cravings of sensuality and existence in order to realize a way out of the dukkha of life. Every insight brings us a bit closer to perfection. Everything is impermanent. We can't hold on to anything, and so nothing is totally satisfying. The meaning of our life is spiritual growth, so that we can eventually give up the ego illusion and live and die unburdened.

Nibbana means "not burning," hence to extinguish. We are all burning, because we want something, because we are discontented, because our passions drive us. Equanimity is one of the factors of enlightenment and means seeing everything in the same light, without advantages or disadvantages. Disenchantment is the first step toward "burning-no-more," the first step beyond this world, and leads us to a complete letting go. Only those who give themselves up can win eternal life. To be sure, nothing is accomplished just by thinking; we also have to be able to grasp what understood experience means. Experience is feeling, and realizing is in the mind.

According to the Buddha's teaching, there are thirty-seven steps on the way to enlightenment: the four foundations of mindfulness, the four great efforts, the Eightfold Path, the five spiritual faculties, the five spiritual forces, the four roads to power, and the seven factors of enlightenment. The seven factors of enlightenment are the final product, while the other thirty steps show us the direction. We have already discussed all these steps, up to the four roads to power. The Buddha said that those who don't make use of these roads to power wouldn't be able to find the path to enlightenment. In Pali these four roads to power are called *iddhipada*. *Pada* is the way, and *iddhi* (corresponding to *siddhi* in Sanskrit) are supernatural powers. The Buddha never denied that such supernatural forces exist. Rather, he explained that an enlightened person can develop and use them for a good purpose, whereas unenlightened persons shouldn't concern themselves with them, because they would be directing their energy along false paths.

These four roads to power are, on the one hand, supernatural forces. But on the other hand they refer to an education of the mind. All four are modes of concentration. The first is the concentration of intention, and means that we shouldn't fritter our lives away; we have to set priorities. The spiritual power of a man or woman is acquired through one-pointedness. When we concentrate all our forces on one point, then there's real power behind it. We have to make it clear to ourselves what's most important and then consistently follow this.

Now, only a very few people can dedicate themselves completely to spiritual development. One's livelihood has to be ensured. The Buddha recommended spending a third of our earnings for ourselves and our family, setting aside another third for bad times, and donating the last third for charitable purposes.

One-pointed intention is then joined by the concentration of willpower. This means that the intention is accompanied by energy. This isn't so simple, because, as the proverb says so beautifully, "The spirit is willing, but the flesh is weak." If we succeed in linking our intention with willpower, we experience purification and contentment. We can clearly recognize intention and willpower right there in meditation. The intention is definitely there, but do we have the willpower to translate it into reality? The same is true of good deeds. The intention is surely always available, but it won't lead to success without the support of willpower.

The third and fourth steps are concentration of consciousness and concentration of deliberation, which means calm and understanding. The two first steps form the prelude and are the building blocks, the next two are results.

Concentration of consciousness means holding one-pointed attention where you have aimed it. Then follows the concentration of deliberation. Wise reflection is an insightful realization, from which dukkha is explored with more and more objectivity. What is dukkha, and where does it come from? Under what conditions does it come about? Where is the "I" to be found? These observations have to be conducted objectively, otherwise the whole thing doesn't work.

Here is a suggestion apropos of the story about the set of teeth: when we admire flowers in the garden, we should quite consciously say to ourselves: "Very pretty. But it doesn't last long!" This way we will eventually get to the point where we observe arising and ceasing with complete equanimity, thereby sparing ourselves a great deal of suffering.

17. PATH AND FRUIT

IF WE HAVE RECOGNIZED in meditation all the things that don't satisfy, the search will be on for what has no cause and no conditions, the search for perfect peace of mind, independent of all circumstances. Since by this time we are familiar with the jhānas, the mind is able to concentrate. But during the jhānas the mind has something to observe, even though the observer in the fourth or fifth jhāna is scarcely recognizable anymore. Nevertheless he or she is still there, and so this state is still not the absolute one. Jhānas are always relative, because there is an observer and something observed. To arrive definitively at letting go, observer and observed must be one. This is a moment that has the quality of meditative absorption, but goes one step above and beyond it, because the observer disappears. This is what I call the "still point," a point of silence at which the mind is no longer in motion.

We have previously determined that the mind moves, whether in absorption or not. It moves, and this movement, however slight, means friction; and friction is dukkha.

To get to the point of stillness and experience it, the "I" and all clinging to it must be fully and intentionally given up. The Buddha said that nibbana is without clinging. Clinging refers first of all to the people who belong to us, and above all to our own "me." This is the strongest kind of clinging: the craving to exist. It arises out of our ignorance with regard to the absolute and brings us nothing but problems. Thus it's necessary to release ourselves through meditation from the five aggregates, of which our ego apparently consists. If we let go of these five aggregates, then at the same time we are setting ourselves free from the five hindrances. The Buddha has given us a parable for this. As he often pointed out, parables are helpful for intelligent people, because a picture can give them a feel for the truth.

He says the following: We are standing on a riverbank, but we're no longer content to be on this side. We have realized that there are nothing but difficulties here, and we also know what they consist in: in our false belief in a "me," which we no longer trust, because we know that it's just an idea that relates to the aggregates and constantly draws us into sensuality. So we'd like to get to the other shore, where stillness rules, as we can tell, thanks to our greater clarity of vision. Now on our shore there is a mighty tree growing, with a bough that juts out over the river. This bough is a symbol of the ego illusion, which is fused into the tree. On the bough of the "me" illusion hangs a rope, which symbolizes our body. We are now willing to risk the leap across the river, for we have already taken all the necessary steps. And we know that this leap will bring us real peace. With the running start of our previous practice we grab the rope and swing across. Now we have to completely let go of our identification with the body and the mind, and let ourselves drop onto the other shore. If we succeed, we don't, of course, immediately land firmly on both feet, because we first have to recover our balance in this new world. That can take some time, but we have in any event achieved what is called, surprisingly, "stream entry." What does that mean? We are now in the stream that leads to nibbana, because we were willing to completely let go of our "self." The event has three results, that is, we have gotten free of the first three of the ten fetters that bind us to the cycle of birth and rebirth.

First, we have extinguished the false view of the ego and momentarily learned how it feels to live without this illusion. Because of that, we now have the right view of "self," and this triggers an interesting phenomenon: the feeling of the not-me, which is called the "path-moment" (*magga*) and is followed by knowledge, the fruit-moment; it disappears again, but the knowledge of the not-me remains with us.

Although this knowledge is great and far-reaching, we have to keep remembering it in order to experience this feeling. Yet we know that we ourselves and all other men and women consist of body and mind and are encumbered with greed and hatred only because of ignorance. The result of this experience will be that we're no longer surprised at all the things done by the human race in general and the people around us in particular. We clearly recognize the false view of the individual ego as the cause of the inner unrest that plagues us all.

The second fetter that we lose is skeptical doubt. We no longer have any doubt that there is only one important task in life: spiritual growth, in order to reach the perfect truth. We no longer harbor any sort of doubt that the Buddha's teaching is really the truth, for we have experienced it ourselves. We no longer doubt that we can follow his directives, because we have already done so. This certainty also relates to our daily life. The skeptical doubt that kept sending us off on some new quest to satisfy our longings has finally been eliminated.

The third fetter that we lose is our belief in rites and rituals, and not just from a religious standpoint. We have now ceased to believe in their ability to lead us to truth. The hard and fast views and opinions about what has to happen and in what exact way simply dissolve. We all have so many of these opinions that we often don't even realize it, but go on acting in accordance with old routines and patterns. We have notions of what other people's images of us should be, of what appearances mean, of how we have to exercise our profession and do our business—in short there is nothing about which we haven't formed an opinion. So long as we haven't seen through impermanence and dukkha, we cling to these opinions, because they support our ego illusion. But now our assumption breaks up that everyone with an opinion different from ours must be wrong. The moment without ego illusion shakes our firmly anchored views and shows us that they're based only on what pleases us.

By now three strong fetters have fallen off, but there has been no mention yet of any lessening of greed and hatred, which are still as powerful as ever. Still, important progress has been made: greed and hatred are seen and recognized more clearly, and this makes our efforts at purification easier. Our cravings in particular are often so thickly veiled that we don't recognize them. But after this step, craving is exposed, and we notice all the unpleasantness and catastrophes of every description that it has hitherto unleashed. Meanwhile we have also learned: recognize, don't blame, change. We'll stride ahead on our path with more willpower and without self-criticism.

We have entered the stream, which means that a person who has taken this step can no longer break the five precepts, because the clear recognition of greed and hatred in his or her own heart would make that too unpleasant. It's likewise said that anyone who has entered the stream will need a maximum of another seven lives before reaching total enlightenment. Of course, the whole path can be completed in one life. On the other hand, all Buddhist meditation masters agree that those who don't reach this point in this lifetime have wasted a good human life. Now the moment has come, following which we can be sure that we will never again fall into lower levels of consciousness. There is only one clear path, and the outside world can no longer touch us as it used to.

The fruit-moment must be followed by a recapitulation in order to integrate the new state of consciousness and determine what actually has changed. In the fruit-moment itself we experience a great relief, as if we had laid down a heavy burden. And that's exactly what has happened, because the ego is burdensome. This feeling won't last long, but we can recall it at will, in order to undertake the next steps. Although the path-moment is only a flash of mental lightning, it's nevertheless an enormous experience that only we ourselves can corroborate. Likewise it's necessary to look more than once to see what has changed in us, and how we will deal with the five hindrances from now on. This self-knowledge requires the greatest sincerity, but henceforth that won't be a problem.

Since we perceive greed and hatred far more clearly now, we also notice our clinging more distinctly, and we have a powerful urge to liberate ourselves from it. Those who are in a position to take the leap from clinging into the unknown for a second time are called once-returners. The leap itself, the letting go of the ego illusion, is the same as it was the first time; but it leads us further into new territory, because we have already had some practice. As the name suggests, such persons need only be reborn one more time in the human realm to attain nibbana. They can, if they have decided to do so, be a great help to the human race. However, they have the choice of whether or not to teach. In recapitulating and recognizing our state of consciousness we notice that greed and hatred still exist, but they have been transformed into "preferences" and "irritation." The way we react when we are challenged in any way provides an especially good way of ascertaining how much we have changed.

After every such step we recognize in the fruit-moment the Four Noble Truths. We see clearly that dukkha comes from our wishing and clinging, and that we have experienced a moment of total freedom. We also know that the Eightfold Path has led us there. This moment is comparable to a sunrise, which pours out warmth and light and extinguishes cold and darkness, so that four results are attained. Despite the wonderful findings, even this step still doesn't bring with it the feeling of non-self. That's acquired only with the final step—the step of full enlightenment. If we keep trying to remember our way back emotionally to the last fruit-moment, it will help us to break through the ego illusion. We'll get a feeling of transparency; the solidity and compactness of the person is shaken, and there arises a feeling of presence without pressure. Every person who harbors the three poisons of greed, hatred, and delusion exercises pressure on himself and on his environment. That's why he or she feels depressed—it's our existential dukkha. It's impossible to cope with this intellectually. When the emotional seeing through of illusion has gotten a stronger hold in us, it will become clear that only extinction brings redemption.

18. Nibbāna without Clinging

THE NON-RETURNER (*anāgāmī*) is called that because he or she never comes back to the human level again. Only those who bear greed and hatred within themselves can live on our level. The non-returner is one step away from enlightenment and has lost the five lower fetters. The first three had already been shed by the stream-enterer. The once-returner lessened greed and hatred, and the non-returner definitely let go of these two. Should we wish to get to know someone who is without greed and hatred, we have to look for a person who stands one step away from enlightenment. The non-returner is reborn on a higher level of consciousness, on a Brahma-level, a divine level. True, the state of consciousness, even on the divine level, is changeable, but it lasts so long that it's perceived as eternal. Such clearsightedness prevails there that beings feel omniscient and almighty. There's such a great difference between this level of consciousness and the human level that these beings can scarcely exert any influence on us. But humans have a chance—through the four brahma-viharas, the divine abodes—to get a glimpse of the divine level and to make contact with it. These higher states of consciousness are called deva-worlds. That means that the devas can deal only with those men and women who have a great deal of loving-kindness in their heart. The others don't "smell good enough" and hence are repellent to the devas.

Of the non-returners it is said that their ego clings to them as the fragrance does to a flower. So it's very subtle, but the five higher fetters still bind him or her to the wheel of birth and death. All these fetters are based on the remnants of the ego illusion. One of them is called ignorance, because the absolute truth hasn't yet been fully integrated. This small amount of clinging is called conceit, in Pali *mano*. It doesn't mean one is conceited; it means one still conceives that one has an ego. It gives rise to the wish for rebirth in a heavenly world. Such persons do not, in fact, feel greed and hatred anymore; their interior life is perfectly harmonious, and they don't want to give it up. They are, admittedly, still exposed to all the difficulties that humans have to confront, but they don't react with rejection or possessiveness.

Since their interior life is so harmonious, they may sense no particularly strong stimulus toward a further step; and when they die, they will find themselves on the levels of divine consciousness. According to the cosmology of the Buddha, there are four such levels, each one more subtle than the other. Now everything depends upon how strong the desire for deliverance of this non-returner is, and whether the eight jhānas have been achieved, in order to determine on which of these four subtle levels they will be reborn.

The subtle ego conceit and the wish for paradise lead to a certain restlessness, though not nearly as much as with people in general. But every wish brings dukkha with it, which explains why the non-returner still has to break free of the five higher fetters in order to attain total freedom.

The first of the higher fetters, then, is ignorance (the subtle clinging to the ego), the second is ego conceit. Then come two fetters that relate to the fact that on the heavenly level one can be reborn in two different types of realms—material and immaterial—both of which are longed for. The last fetter is restlessness. When a person reaches such a stage, he or she will know all about this unrest or restlessness. If he or she is physically strong enough, that person will surely try to gain complete freedom. It's not unusual for someone who has gotten so far to be fairly old and no longer physically capable of meditating properly. But it's quite possible for a young person to reach this stage.

Non-returners can live in the state of non-ego by directing their mindfulness to it. They can recognize this void within them by concentrating on it and reacting accordingly. But constant non-ego awareness is lacking as much now as ever, because there is still a job to be done. If such a person can continue to meditate and practice, he or she will likely succeed in taking the next step. In principle it's simply a matter of breaking the first of the five fetters, because the other four are nothing but the result of ignorance about the ego illusion, a remnant of which still exists. This is where the wishes for paradise come from.

If such persons now continue to practice, they will continually recognize themselves—and that's the point. The further one goes along this path, the more it will come down to a continuous self-scrutiny. This inner scrutiny will become increasingly impersonal, because one faces oneself much more objectively. Through constant practice it becomes a habit and lets even non-returners recognize the little blockages in their hearts.

We all have blockages in our hearts, built up of worry, craving, wishes, ingrained opinions, rejections, and uncertainties. Non-returners, of course, may not find all this anymore, but they discern that somewhere in their heart a certain heaviness and a certain clinging still remain. This shows them that they have to risk taking yet another leap. The image of jumping off naturally shouldn't serve as a visual, imaginary replacement for effective letting go. With the next step one must do something quite extraordinary: let go of everything spiritual, mental, and material, and in the truest sense of the word give up oneself fully and completely, dissolve into the suchness of the universe, where there are no separate manifestations of any kind. This willingness is followed by a moment of total concentration in which the detaching of oneself can take place. The result in the next moment is not just relief, as before, but also awareness of the collapse of all the blockages that have ever existed. Here too the feeling arises of entering new territory, but accompanied now by the certainty that one has come home.

A person who has followed his or her path this far has no more obscurities and can clearly see that he or she has abandoned the ego illusion. Such a person is called an Arahat (Skt. *arhat*)—an Enlightened One. He or she creates no more kamma, because there now exist only mind and body, without ego.

Actions can no longer produce results, because no one is there to experience the results.

For forty-five years the Buddha taught every day, in all weather, in sickness and in health. He acted out of compassion for all living beings that keep having to suffer because of the ego illusion.

The energy of enlightenment is the strongest energy available in the universe. When we devote ourselves to the Buddha's teaching as our stimulus and guideline, and to daily meditation, this enlightenment energy may be experienced personally. Before his death the Buddha recommended making a pilgrimage to the places where he lived and worked. Bodhgaya, the place of his enlightenment, is today a place of pilgrimage for millions of people who come to the bodhi tree, under which the Buddha sat and meditated. The original tree no longer exists; it was destroyed by Muslims during a religious war. Today there stands a sprout from the bodhi tree from Sri Lanka, which in turn grew from a sprout taken from the original tree. In going around the stūpa it seemed to me as if the ground was charged with energy and was filling my whole body with it. As I made the round, the fatigue of the trip fell away from me, and a deep silence gripped my heart. Thus I sat down to meditate after walking around the stūpa, and all eighty members of the travel group did the same, although some of them had never meditated before in their lives and no one had encouraged them to do so.

Later I spoke with several women who had found the energy prevailing there almost uncanny and who wondered why they had sensed practically none of it in Lumbini. Suddenly it occurred to me that when he was in Lumbini the Buddha wasn't enlightened yet, whereas here in Bodhgaya and where he died in Kushinara, in the fullness of his enlightenment, people who weren't at all practiced in meditation became concentrated immediately and had no difficulties whatsoever with meditation.

Another interesting thing happened in Kushinara. When I had taken a few steps around the stūpa there, I smelled sandalwood and thought that someone walking behind me had just lit a stick of incense. I turned around, but I was quite alone. Then I waited a few moments to see whether anyone with a joss stick might not show up after all. There was a wonderful aroma, and after a few moments a friend came by. As she approached, she asked whether I had burned a stick, because it smelled so pleasant. Later it occurred to us that the Buddha and other Enlightened Ones had earlier been cremated on a pyre of sandalwood. From these experiences I concluded that the energy of enlightenment doesn't get lost, that it's at the disposal of anyone who opens up to it. We can compare this to a radio broadcast. If our receivers are turned on and we have the right wavelength, we'll hear the transmission.

King Ajātasattu was very pleased with the Buddha's explanations and now wanted to become a follower. After the Buddha had accepted him as a disciple, the king finally confessed his terrible deed, the murder of his father, whereupon the Buddha told him that merely deciding that he wished to follow the Buddha had many advantages. When the king had gone away, the Buddha said to his monks that Ajātasattu would now be a stream-enterer if he hadn't murdered his father. But this deed had created an insurmountable block, and the consequences simply had to be borne. And so it was. Ajātasattu was murdered by his son, and the patricide was repeated five times in the royal house. Finally, the people had enough of it, and they killed the last king, in order to choose a brand-new one.

The Buddha compared enlightenment to an extremely sharp-eyed person who stands in front of a clear lake and can plainly make out what's on the bottom. This remark was sometimes misunderstood, and the Buddha was asked if he were omniscient. His answer was always "no." His nephew and attendant Ānanda then wanted an explanation of why the Buddha didn't consider himself omniscient. The Buddha said that he always knew what his mindfulness was directed to, but naturally he didn't know what his mindfulness was *not* directed to.

If we turn our mindfulness to the spiritual teachings and direct our attention this way, if we're always aware of what dukkha is, and choose liberation from it, our mind inclines toward spiritual growth. This is the task presented to those who are on a spiritual path. If we are applying our practice of meditation simply to put a more pleasant face on our world, that expectation will be disappointed. Meditation is designed to purify the mind and to strengthen us in the knowledge that we can transcend the things of this world.

After his enlightenment, the Buddha sat for a whole week in the happiness and joy of experiencing nibbana. In the process he distanced himself with his mind from all worldly things. That doesn't necessarily mean that he entered into the jhānas, although that was the case now and then. He simply left behind him everything that exists in the world. He experienced the joy and happiness of the awakened state without any clinging, because his ego had dissolved. Then he could go back into the world in order to let it share in the good that he bore within himself. Although he was touched by worldly circumstances, his mind never wavered again. The world is still there, admittedly, but the Enlightened One moves in it only to help.

Enlightenment is the highest state that a person can ever attain. A deep contentment and joy, along with serenity, make him or her completely independent of the world, because the world is built on an illusion. In Hinduism that is called *māyā*, in Pali *moha*. It's hard to comprehend what this illusion consists in, since we believe that if we can take hold of something, it must exist. But the illusion consists in the fact that we view what we take hold of or can grasp with the other senses as the only existing reality. We want to find inner peace, spiritual growth, and eternal happiness in the world. But neither the world nor human beings can give us that, because it's all just the backdrop of the play in which we are the actors. We identify ourselves with our costumes (which we're constantly changing), so that we fit in with the play being put on at the moment. Shakespeare wrote, "All the world's a stage, and all the men and women merely players." He knew about spiritual values, otherwise his work would not have become immortal.

The illusion consists exclusively in our view of things. The Enlightened One sees everything quite differently, and even on the way to enlightenment the field of vision changes. Knowledge doesn't hit us like a lightning bolt; it's comparable to a slow ascent, until on the mountain peak the air becomes pure and the view crystal-clear. Afterward life will run, to outward appearances, exactly as it did before, but inwardly it will be transformed.

Sāriputta, the Buddha's close disciple, said in a discourse that all those who announced their enlightenment to him had come to it in one of the following three ways. Either they first acquired understanding and then concentration, or first concentration and then understanding, or they worked on both at the same time. It's not important which one we get to first. Our understanding of this way is what counts, not the hope of results.

When the Buddha spoke about his enlightenment, and when anyone else explained his or her own enlightenment experience, they often ended by saying:

Destroyed is birth;
the holy life has been lived.
What had to be done has been done;
there is nothing further beyond this.

QUESTIONS AND ANSWERS

Q: Can children also create kamma?
A: Yes. They say that from around the age of two it's possible. Before then the intention isn't clear yet—it's still a matter of instinct. But at the age of two thinking and acting intentionally is possible, and intention always makes kamma.

Q: I'm of the opinion that the jhānas are a question of energy, that energy keeps getting used so that you can give yourself completely.
A: Of course, we're talking about mental energy here.

Q: Can one promote this with any physical or mental exercises?
A: Yes. Through constant mindfulness. Here the word

"constant" has to be used carefully. It's better to say "as constantly as possible." Anyone who isn't enlightened can't be continuously mindful. Everything in life has to be observed mindfully, above all, body and mind. This brings out the energy needed for concentration, which in turn creates more fresh energy. A mind that is not mindful wanders off into the distance and can't orient itself to one point.

Q: Isn't that very strenuous?

A: No one ever claimed that it isn't. Things as easy, for example, as turning on the TV can be mastered by any child. But where does that get you? Things that our mind finds strenuous are what bring profit. People who complete a course of studies have to strain, otherwise they won't get their diploma and can't earn a living.

What we gain on the spiritual path is eternity. And that is surely laborious. You could call the spiritual way the university of the mind. Meditation and the whole path are a training of the mind, where meditation is the science of the mind. If that weren't the case, nobody could be helped through meditation. But because it's a science, it always produces, in an altogether concrete way, the same experiences, so that everyone goes the same way. True, the Buddha describes this somewhat differently, but that doesn't matter, since it's merely a question of words.

Q: Couldn't one employ chakra or yoga exercises for this kind of energy work? The yogis practice that too in order to attain the absorptions.

A: Yoga exercises are extremely helpful, since they teach proper sitting. You learn to stretch your limbs. Every type of exercise that promotes concentration is helpful. In the teaching of the Buddha the focus is more on contemplations that concern the whole body and not just individual points.

Q: Practicing mindfulness causes joy, even when the contemplations relate to anicca. I find that this has nothing to do with effort and sadness. Only when I notice that my mindfulness is slipping does some of my joy get lost.

A: That's correct. But you are already experienced in it, because you've been practicing for quite a while now; so the mind has gotten used to it and is perfectly aware that it's a question of the right way. The untrained person must intentionally turn away from his or her sensual drives, to gain mindfulness. That's hard work. By contrast, the person who has practiced knows that this mindfulness is the only thing that guarantees a harmonious and peaceful course of life.

Q: The phrase "the wheel of dhamma" gives the impression that the teaching rolls on like a wheel.

A: Correct! It rolled—and it's still rolling. That's what that means.

Q: The murder that the king committed had to be repeated, no? So do you keep having to have a perpetrator?

A: When someone has killed his own father, it's already highly probable that he will be killed too. But not necessarily by his son.

Q: Still, is it true, that evil always draws evil after it? Is it an endless process?

A: Yes, there will always be a villain. The world is full of misdeeds.

Q: But what if no one reacted to evil actions?

A: In this world with its billions of people should there be just good ones? Is that the question?

Q: Yes. If nobody reacted to evil, then everybody would necessarily be purified.

A: And you want to know if that's possible? We can't expect that. We already have enough problems, although we're making an effort. And with most people there isn't even any effort.

LOVING-KINDNESS MEDITATION

Please put your attention on your breath for a few moments.

Now we wish to open our hearts and give ourselves to love, which is a feeling of warmth and devotion, of accepting and enfolding and embracing. This self-giving in love is something we wish to lay claim to, in order to present ourselves with it.

Now we turn in loving devotion to the person who is sitting closest to us, and enfold and fill this person with the warmth of our hearts and devotion and accept him or her completely. We shower this person with loving feelings.

Now we turn in loving devotion to all those present and fill and enfold them with the warmth of our hearts and devotion. We accept them the way they are, we judge and condemn no one, but simply accept them in our hearts.

Now we turn in loving devotion to our parents, full of warmth, devotion, and acceptance. We take them into our hearts.

Now we think of those nearest and dearest to us, perhaps those with whom we live, and give them our hearts without expecting to get the same thing in return. We also open our hearts to them and let them in. We don't judge or condemn, but enfold these people with devotion and warmth.

Now we open our hearts as wide as possible and let the loving devotion flow forth to all people, near and far, to those we know and those we don't know, those of whom we have heard or whose existence we can only guess. Loving devotion is like a jewel in which everyone can have a share. We only need to let it flow, then it will reach many hearts.

We now let this jewel of loving devotion radiate within us until there is not a single cell without warmth, devotion, acceptance, and dedication. We feel ourselves made happy and protected by it and fasten this jewel in our hearts, so that we can have access to it at any time.

INDEX

illusion: "me" as, 51, 118, 153; the world as, 199

impermanence, 84, 123; accepting, 169–70; and equanimity, 138; investigating, 84–85, 123; and loving-kindness, 167–68; recalling, 101, 125. *See also* arising and ceasing

indifference: equanimity vs., 65, 125, 137

individuality, 175

inefficacy of action: doctrine of, 4–5, 5–7, 40

infinite consciousness, 115–16

infinite space: feeling of, 114–15

injustice: kamma and, 129

insecurity: acceptance of, 182; material things and, 42–43

insight, *30*, 81, 123; into absolute truth, 116, 117–18; concentration and, 122, 123, 184; and devotion, 44; into the five aggregates, 123–26; fruits of knowledge, *30–37*, 190, 192; the jhānas and, 106, 109, 122, 123; and serenity, 143, 166. *See also* clear comprehension; seeing

instinct, 67

insubstantiality, 117; investigating, 85, 86, 123

intellect. *See* rational mind

intention, 91; concentration of, 187; to meditate, 91; right intention, 155–56

interconnectedness: contemplating, 72–73

interpersonal relations, 131–42, 162–65, 171, 172, 178

intoxicants: not consuming, 54, 110

"iron eagle," 46

irritation: hatred as transformed into, 192

jewel image, 122

jhānas (absorptions), 95–97, 100–20, 175; 1st (*See* rapture); 2nd (joy), *28*, 103, 106, 111–12; 3rd (peace), *29*, 108–10, 112; 4th (equanimity), *29–30*, 110–11, 112; 5th (infinite space), 114–15; 6th (infinite consciousness), 115–16; 7th

(emptiness), 118–19; 8th (no perception/nonperception), 119; entrance into, 95–97; fine-material absorptions, 95, 100–13, 111–12, 166; immaterial absorptions, 114–20; influence of, 106–7, 120, 175, 181; and insight, 106, 109, 122, 123; mastery of, 119–20; as mental states, 106, 189; purification through, 96, 104, 110, 118, 147–48; vs. trance, 119

journey: as what matters, 90

joy, 102–3, 106, 111–12, 199; and concentration, 106, 109; mindfulness and, 201–2; purification of, 97; sympathetic, 136–37. *See also* happiness; rapture

judgment: and love, 132–33

Kaccāyana, Pakudha, 2; doctrine of, *8–9*

kamma, 127–29; creation of, 128–29, 131, 174, 200; as impersonal, 129

Kassapa, Pūraṇa, *1*; doctrine of, *4–5*

Kesakambala, Ajita, 2; doctrine of, *7–8*

khandas. *See* five aggregates

killing, 47–48

knowledge, 80, 199–200; fruits of, *30–37*, 190, 192; of the not-me, 190. *See also* clear comprehension; insight; understanding

Komārabhacca, Jīvaka, 2, *3*, 39, 40

Kushinara, 197–98

ladle and can images, 171–72

laziness. *See* mental laziness

leap of letting go, 190, 192–93, 196

leaves image, 175–76

leaving of home, *13–14*, *15*, 41–42

letting go, 125, 136, 145, 165; of desires, 49–51, 76–77, 104–6, 108, 151–52, 153, 159–68; of the ego, 96–97, 101–2, 112, 125–26, 144–45, 189–93; leap of, 190, 192–93, 196; at the moment of death, 125–26; parable of, 189–90; of peace, 110; sinking into ourselves, 108. *See also* abandoning; equanimity

liberation. *See* enlightenment

lies image, 172
limiting: possessions, 162; sense contacts,
   24–25, 57–65, 159–61; thinking, 58–
   59, 60–65, 137–38
livelihood: abstaining from debased arts,
   21–24; allocating earnings, 187; freedom from work, 13–14, 41–42; right
   livelihood, 174
lobha, 134
"looking at the field of corpses," 73
looking inside ourselves, 60, 68
lotus pond image, 29, 110
love, 48–49, 76, 132–35, 139, 146; as
   craving, 134; desire to be loved, 48,
   49–51; dislike as preferred to, 80; and
   doubt, 93–94; enemies of (See clinging; hatred); in equanimity, 137; and
   fear of death, 48–49; and freedom,
   48; and fulfillment, 48; and generosity,
   51; independent vs. dependent,
   132–34; and killing/harming, 48–49;
   and meditation, 135; motherly love,
   134, 139–40, 141–42; as practice, 132;
   practicing, 51–52, 140–41; reacting
   with, 135; and self-confidence, 135;
   true love, 49, 135. See also compassion;
   loving-kindness
loving-kindness (metta), 49, 134; and
   boundaries, 52; and consciousness,
   115–16; and impermanence, 167–68.
   See also compassion; love
loving-kindness contemplation, 55–56
loving-kindness meditation, 97, 98–99,
   203
luxuries: abstaining from, 19
lying. See not speaking falsely

man from Rājagaha: the Buddha and,
   112–13
mango taste, 44
material things. See things
"me": clinging to, 189; as an illusion, 51,
   118, 153; investigation of, 125,
   180–81; nonexistence in the body, 69,
   71; submergence, 111; as trouble-
   maker, 184–85. See also ego; self

means: reflections on, 67–68
medicine: of the Buddha, 166–67
meditation, 59, 65, 89, 180; absorptions
   in (See jhānas); aspects (directions),
   143, 166; conditions for, 181; vs. contemplation, 55; equanimity and, 138;
   and everyday life, 83; first step (opening the door), 94–95; foundations of,
   100; immediate results, 91–92, 94, 100;
   insight in (See insight); intention to
   meditate, 91; interest in, 95; investigating the three characteristics of existence, 85–86; letting go in, 96–97;
   love and, 135; loving-kindness meditation, 97, 98–99, 203; overcoming the
   hindrances in, 92, 94, 95–96; purpose
   of, 110; restlessness in (See restlessness); and self-confidence, 45; and
   sensual desires, 106, serenity in (See
   serenity); sticking with the object of,
   92–94; turning to the object of, 91–92;
   walking meditation, 70–71. See also
   concentration; mindfulness; practice
mental attitudes: examining, 77–78. See
   also mental states; perceptions
mental formations, 81, 123; investigating, 125. See also reactions; thought
   content
mental laziness (dullness), 26, 91–92
mental states (moods), 182; examining,
   82–83; jhānas as, 106; mindfulness
   (See mindfulness); mindfulness of, 64,
   78–83; negative (See negative states)
mettā. See loving-kindness
Middle Way, 123, 126, 152
mind: aspects (See five aggregates); clarity, 29, 111, 126; concentration of (See
   concentration); directing (See directing the mind); encompassing the
   minds of others, 33; heart and, 43–44;
   laziness, 26, 91–92; liberation of (See
   enlightenment); rational mind, 43;
   states (See mental states); wandering
   (See restlessness). See also consciousness; thinking; thoughts
mind objects, 86

mind-made body: knowledge of, *30–31*

mindfulness, 29, 82, 84, 89, 165–66; acting with, 25; of the body, 64, 69–75;
boredom in practicing, 87; and clear
comprehension, 66, 69; and concentration, 174–75; and energy, 200–1; of
feelings, 64, 76–78; foundations of, 64,
69–87; importance of, 62, 76, 82; and
joy, 201–2; and knowledge, 80; of
mental states, 64, 78–83; outward vs.
inward, 74–75; persevering in, 87; and
the precepts, 54; right mindfulness,
175; as stressful, 88; of thought content, 64, 83–87. *See also* contemplation; meditation

mirror images, *33*, 75, 172, 173

monastic rules, *15–24*

moods. *See* mental states

moral behavior (renunciation): fourfold
restraint doctrine, *9–10*, 41; guardians
of, 163; monastic rules, *15–24*; the
precepts, *15–16*, 47–56; rapture and,
97; self-discipline, 54, 92; steps on the
Eightfold Path, 154–55, 170–74; and
trust, 42

mosquitos: not killing, 177

motherly love, 134, 139–40, 141–42

movement (movements): of the body:
observing, 69–70; and dukkha, 170,
189; of everything, 124

mudra: open left hand, 176

murder, 202

Nātaputta, Nigaṇṭha, 2; doctrine of,
9–10

negative states, 78–81; dislike as preferred to love, 80; and feelings, 80;
recognizing, 78–79; response formula,
79, 135; scapegoating others, 80–81;
triggers of, 79; trying to change, 83.
See also mental states

negative thoughts. *See* unwholesome
thoughts

nibbāna, 160, 186; foretaste of, 106. *See
also* enlightenment

noble conversation, 53–54, 104, 173

noble friends, 104, 164

non-ego state, 195–96

non-returners, 194–96

nonprofession: doctrine of, *10–11*, 41

nonself, 84, 123; examination of, 180–81;
feeling of, 193; non-ego state, 195–96.
See also insubstantiality

not consuming intoxicants, 54, 110

not killing/not harming, *15–16, 17*,
47–51; contemplation of, 55, 56; love
and, 48–49; mosquitos, 177

not sexually misusing others, 52; abstaining from intercourse, *16*

not speaking falsely, *16, 19–20*, 52–54,
170–73, 177

not taking what's not given, *16*, 51–52

not-me: feeling of, 190; knowledge of,
190–91

observing: power of, 59, 64, 82–83

once-returners, 192–93

opening of the heart, 43, 44, 134

order: putting things in, 45

others: clinging to, 134–35; condemning,
75, 132; encompassing the minds of,
33; loving, 140–41; observing, 75;
scapegoating, 80–81; suffering abuse
from, 128

ourselves: finding out about, 81–82;
looking inside, 60, 68; as mental proc-
esses, 81; pressure on, 146–47, 193; reactions as harmful to, 131; refusing to
be victims, 79; seeing for, 85, 112–13;
sinking into, 108

Padmasambhava: prophecy, 46

paradise: wishes for, 195, 196

passing away and reappearance of beings: seeing, *35–36*. *See also* arising
and ceasing

past lives: knowledge of recollecting, *34*

path. *See* Eightfold Path; spiritual path

path-moment, 190, 192

patience, 44, 68, 89–91

peace, 108–10, 112; letting go of, 110. *See
also* equanimity; serenity

seeing: feelings arising from, 57–58; limiting, 58; for ourselves, 85, 112–13; the
passing away and reappearance of beings, 35–36; things as they are, 81, 90–
91. See also insight
self: right view of, 190. See also ego;
"me"; nonself; ourselves
self-blame, 41, 68
self-confidence, 28, 106; love and, 135;
and meditation, 45; trust and, 45, 93
self-discipline, 54, 86, 92
self-examination (self-scrutiny), 81–82,
125, 179–80, 180–81, 196
sense contacts, 57, 81, 123; ascertaining,
78; causal connections, 82, 124, 127;
and feelings, 57–58, 78; limiting, 24–
25, 57–65, 159–61. See also hearing;
seeing
sensual desires, 36, 151, 157, 159; overcoming, 49–51, 76–77, 104–6, 108,
151–52, 153, 159–68
sensuality, craving of, 36, 151–52, 153,
157, 159
separation (of partners), 141, 178
serenity (calm), 166, 199; and insight,
143, 166. See also peace
serenity (samatha) meditation, 86
set of teeth story, 185–86
seven bodies: doctrine of, 8–9, 40–41
seven factors of enlightenment, 84, 86,
165–66
sex: abstaining from intercourse, 16; not
misusing others, 52; sex drive, 151
Shakespeare, William, 199
shame: and moral behavior, 163
sickness image, 26
silence of mind, 111; still point, 189
six roots, 146, 147, 184
six teachers: doctrines of, 4–11, 40–41
skandhas. See five aggregates
skeptical doubt. See doubt
skilled worker images, 32
slavery: freedom from, 12–13, 41
slavery image, 26–27, 103
sleep: mindfulness during, 87
sloth. See mental laziness

slowing down our reactions, 67, 82
soap-powder ball image, 27–28, 100
soul: seven bodies doctrine, 8–9, 40–41
sounds: hearing divine and human
sounds, 32
speech: feelings and, 53. See also right
speech
"sphere of no-thingness," 118
spider web image, 128
spiritual path, 49, 145; awareness of,
179–80; as laborious, 155, 201; recapitulating the way, 101, 192, 193; swimming against the current, 183–84. See
also Eightfold Path
states of mind. See mental states; negative states
still point, 189
stream enterer, 192, 194
stream entry, 190
submergence in the sea image, 185
suffering. See dukkha
suicidal monk story, 54
Sujata: and the Buddha, 182–83
supernatural powers: four roads to
power, 186–88; knowledge of, 31–32
survival. See craving: for existence
swimming against the current, 183–84
sympathetic joy, 136–37

Tathāgata, 14–15. See also Buddha
teacher: trust in, 43. See also six teachers
teachings of the Buddha, 92–93, 126;
distinguishing aspects, 181; on lying,
171–72; as medicine, 166–67; three
parts, 154–55
teeth story, 185–86
temptation, 160
ten fetters: getting free of, 190–96
Teresa of Ávila, 137
things: analyzing, 84, 105–6, 166; clinging to, 64; and insecurity, 42–43; limiting possessions, 162; putting in
order, 45; seeing as they are, 81, 90–91
thinking, 57, 59, 76, 94; absolutist thinking, 126; feelings arising from, 60; as
habitual, 66; limiting, 58–59, 60–65,

137–38; rest from, 59, 111, 112, 119. *See also* consciousness; thoughts

thought content: mindfulness of, 64, 83–84; shaping, 84–87

thoughts: and action, 174; believing, 64, 83; content, 64, 83–87; and feelings, 60, 76; observing, 59, 64, 82–83; recognizing negative thoughts, 61–63, 91, 165. *See also* thinking; unwholesome thoughts; wholesome thoughts

three characteristics of existence, 84, 123

three cravings (cankers), 150–58, 159–60, 168; knowledge of the destruction of, 36–37; letting go of, 159–68

three roots of unwholesomeness (poisons), 146, 147, 184, 193

three roots of wholesomeness, 146, 147, 184

throwing coals image, 96, 128

time required for enlightenment, 86–87, 192, 193

torpor. *See* mental laziness

trance: vs. the jhānas, 119

transience. *See* impermanence

true love, 49, 135

trust (faith), *15*, 42–46; vs. blind faith, 43; vs. doubt, 93; and the heart, 43; and self-confidence, 45, 93; in the teacher, 43; in trying things out, 44; and wisdom, 43

truth: relative and absolute, 69–70, 116, 117–18. *See also* Four Noble Truths; right speech

trying things out, 44; as enough, 70–71

understanding: of craving, 58; dissolution of assumptions, 191; of the Four Noble Truths, *36*, 193; right understanding, 155. *See also* clear comprehension; insight; knowledge

"unfolding." *See* seven factors of enlightenment

unhappiness: defending against, 79

universe. *See* world

unwholesome thoughts: power, 148; recognizing, 61–63, 91, 165; replacing, 165; response formula, 62; response options, 61

upekkhā. *See* equanimity

urgency: focusing, 146; moment of, 150, 155, 156, 157

"using" our blessings, 161–62

vegetarian diet, 176–77

victims: refusing to be, 79

village travels image, *34*

vipassanā. *See* insight

walking meditation, 70–71

wandering in the desert images, 27, 93, 111–12

wandering mind. *See* restlessness

water element, 71–72

water of life image, 111–12

waves in the ocean image, 51

weeds image, 102–3

wheel of dhamma, 202

white cloth image, *29–30*, 111

wholesome thoughts: pursuing into action, 66–69; response options, 61, 64

willpower. *See* energy

wisdom, 146; arising of, 81, 150; steps on the Eightfold Path, 154–56; and trust, 43. *See also* insight

wise reflection, 150, 153, 164, 174, 188

working. *See* livelihood

world (universe): acceptance of, 159; building an ideal world, 137–38; as illusion, 199; sensory contacts as, 57. *See also* existence

yoga exercises, 201

Zen story: deathbed words, 153